MW01281740

DIGITAL MARKETING OUTSOURCING

The Ultimate Recipe for Growing Your Business Online

Husam Jandal

Contents

Chapter 3
Best Practices for Finding, Hiring, and Managing Freelancers

Chapter 4
The Cost of Outsourcing Digital Marketing Activities

Chapter 5
Climbing the Digital Marketing Tree

Chapter 6
Should You Outsource Digital Marketing Management or Keep it In-House?

Chapter 7
Content Marketing Calendar: What it is and
Why You Need One 65

Chapter 8
Project Management Platforms 77

Chapter 9
Password Management 93

Chapter 10
How to NOT Waste Money on Content Marketing

Chapter 11
Should You Outsource Copywriting or Keep it In-House?

Chapter 12
Should You Outsource Social Media Marketing or Keep it In-House?

Chapter 13
Should You Outsource Your Search Engine Optimization or Keep it In-House?

Chapter 14

Should You Outsource Pay-Per-Click or Keep it In-House?

Chapter 15

Chapter 16

Chapter 17

Chapter 18

Website Hosting - Your Weakest Digital Marketing Link!

Chapter 19

Should You Outsource Video Production or Keep it In-House?

Chapter 20

Should You Outsource Digital Marketing Analytics or Keep it In-House?

Chapter 21

Metrics to Measure Your Marketing Success

Chapter 22
Advantages of Digital Marketing Outsourcing ...221

Chapter 23
Disadvantages of Digital Marketing
Outsourcing 229

Chapter 24
7 Essential Traits of a Marketing Strategist...... 239

Conclusion
Should You Outsource Digital Marketing or
Keep it In-House? 249

About the Author................... 264

Introduction

The Diversity and Complexity of Digital Marketing

There were a little more than two million websites across the globe when Google launched in 1998[i]. It was a golden age. You may remember AOL and Yahoo chatrooms popping up around this point. This was roughly when Netflix emerged too, only the company had to mail physical copies of DVDs back then.

This is the early Internet that I remember as well. I entered the field as a business and marketing consultant in 2000. Nobody had heard the term "digital marketing" at the time. It didn't exist. When a company wanted to take advantage of the World Wide Web, it simply hired someone to create a website and would instantly have an online presence. There was an explosion of web design companies as a result.

Even the way Google operated was different. Its original name was "BackRub" because it focused on backlinks to determine which websites were important[ii]. These days, it looks at hundreds of quality signals[iii]. The proprietary algorithm it uses to determine which sites to serve up and in what order to serve them is updated as many as 600 times per year[iv]. It must adapt. The Internet is constantly evolving.

Whereas simply having a site once worked, there are now thousands of social media platforms, review sites, and places to host online profiles. As a professional, I've seen layer after layer added and watched the landscape become considerably more complicated. Whether you own an SME or are a stakeholder in one, I know you've seen this shift too.

Web designers have also seen the shift. Whereas they once purely marketed themselves as development and design companies, they now market themselves as full-service digital marketing agencies. The problem is that, although they've shifted their branding, they have not shifted their focus. As a result, many still only really know one core area even though they provide a wide range of services.

This is something I've watched from the inside over decades. Not only have I served companies as a business and digital marketing consultant, but I've worked for Google as an educator. I helped marketing professionals become certified experts in things like search, mobile, video, display, and shopping advertising through the Google Partners program. Rigorous training like this makes firms more well-rounded, but few agencies undergo it.

This experience, engaging with both agencies and business owners while actively working in digital marketing, has given me a unique perspective that I'm often asked to share with groups of business owners. I network with people after these events, and, almost without fail, I'm approached by someone with more holistic concerns after each event. While the wording varies, questions fall into a few common themes:

How can I take advantage of all the digital resources available now?

I've had bad experiences with agencies. How can I do it better this time around?

I've poured so much money into digital marketing and not gotten a return or my return has been low. How can I improve my ROI?

What digital marketing tactics should I be engaging in?

I always tell them the same thing: "You need the right recipe." Then, I share my recipe with them.

Over the decades of my career, I've exploited every digital marketing methodology, from planning to strategy and execution. However, I've focused on one methodology and have a 100 percent success rate with it.

My clients are spread across virtually all industries. They're structured in unique ways and operate differently. They have distinct backstories and goals. The commonality they share is that they've followed my recipe for digital marketing success. Many become lifelong friends after our time working together too.

To this day, I receive vacation and travel photos from a business owner I worked with years ago. His 20-year company was bringing in $500 million annually when we first met. The company broke the billion-dollar mark two years into our business relationship. My client sold it, entered early retirement, and is living his dream. That's how well my approach works.

I don't think my methodology should be reserved only for people like him or those who retain me or attend one of my speaking events, though. I think anyone who wants to apply my tested methodology should be able to, and I believe anyone can achieve the same level of success with it too.

My recipe is simple: keep control of your digital marketing efforts in-house, at the heart of your business. Then, ensure every role and channel is handled by a qualified, experienced professional specializing in that area. The latter can almost always be done through outsourcing. Virtually everything else falls into place on its own when you do this. Again, as a business and digital marketing consultant, I've exclusively used this recipe after trying every conceivable alternative and have had a 100 percent success rate with it.

Knowing the basis of the recipe is only one part of the equation, though. You also need to understand how to bring the ingredients together. This book will teach you how.

[i] Internet Live Stats. (N.D.). "Total Number of Websites." Internet Live Stats. https://bit.ly/dmo-Intro-i

[ii] Olivia Waring. "Why is Google called Google?" Metro. https://bit.ly/dmo-Intro-ii

[iii] Andrea Stein. "Your Cheat Sheet to Google's 200 (Known) Ranking Factors." HubSpot. https://bit.ly/dmo-Intro-iii

[iv] Search Engine Land. (N.D.). "Google SEO news: Google algorithm updates." Search Engine Land. https://bit.ly/dmo-Intro-iv

Chapter 1

How Businesses are Investing in Digital Marketing Today

The way companies view digital marketing is shifting. Around 70 percent of all businesses are integrating digital in most of their marketing activities to attract potential customers[i]. The number has remained mostly static even though there's been a four percent drop in companies that see themselves as digital-first organizations in just a few years. In other words, the vast majority see the various digital marketing tactics as an investment, and it's been that way for years, but there's a shift in which vehicles people are using to drive their investments.

Companies are Increasing Their Investment

A recent survey finds business owners are planning to increase their marketing budget by nearly 9 percent year on year[ii]. Budgets follow the continued trend of allocating more for their digital marketing plan, with almost 12 percent growth in digital marketing spending over the past decade and consistent losses across non-digital channels. This is supported by sales increases through digital channels, which amount to 13.4 percent across the board but rise as high as 29 percent in areas like B2C services.

Naturally, when there are percentages involved, there's a high variance in actual spending. In terms of dollars, 81 percent of companies invest at least $50,000 annually on digital marketing, with 41 percent investing at least $500,000[iii].

There's a Move from Paid Channels to Organic Options

Research shows that nearly three-quarters of companies are cutting back on at least one digital marketing channel[iv]. The channels most likely to see decreased budgets and activities are display and banner advertisements and pay-per-click (PPC) campaigns. This may be because targeting and analytics require a specialized skill set, something companies struggle to bring in-house. However, the emergence of marketing technology, or MarTech, makes managing everything from social media platforms like Facebook, Twitter, LinkedIn, Instagram, and YouTube through Search Engine Optimization (SEO) much more straightforward, empowering brands to dominate on specific marketing channels and giving more control over the face being presented.

Digital Marketing Spend is Being Allocated Based Upon Customer Needs

Rather than trying to grow into new products or tap into new markets with their digital marketing plans, CMOs say they're dedicated to enhancing market penetration and serving their existing customer base better. Buyer personas make it easier for organizations to create a content marketing plan to see who they need to cater to and how to tailor it to their customers' needs and get an edge over competitors. This includes content such as blog posts, infographics, and ebooks.

External Resources Are Being Tapped into More

Nearly 60 percent of CMOs said they were moving away from traditional marketing methods and developed new marketing capabilities primarily through in-house training just two years ago. It's now down to 53.8 percent. Today's companies are developing marketing skills by:

- Partnering with other marketing agencies (17.1 percent)
- Partnering with consultancies (13.9 percent)
- Partnering with other companies (12.2 percent)
- Buy other companies (3 percent)
- Companies That Invest More Earn More

Your Digital Marketing Journey May Be Different

It's helpful to know what other companies are doing to get a better feel for benchmarks and industry standards as you begin strategizing, but it's important to note this isn't the end-all. For example, Salesforce, a company dedicated to helping organizations boost sales, has historically devoted more than 40 percent of revenue to digital marketing efforts[v]. They've seen it bring in a total of nearly $10 million in profit this year, with revenue climbing 26 percent year on year. Companies like Oracle, Google, Johnson & Johnson, and Grand Canyon University all have similar stories. Monitor your progress and follow the path that makes the most sense for your business.

[i] Adobe. "Digital Trends." Adobe.com.
https://bit.ly/dmo-1-i

[ii] Deloitte. "August - CMO Survey."
https://bit.ly/dmo-1-ii

[iii] Kristen Herhold. "How Businesses Invest in Digital Marketing." https://bit.ly/dmo-1-iii

[iv] Kristen Herhold. "How Businesses Invest in Digital Marketing." The Manifest. https://bit.ly/dmo-1-iv

[v] Salesforce. "Annual Report: Celebrating 20 Years of Sales." Salesforce.com. https://bit.ly/dmo-1-v

Chapter 2

What Your Digital Marketing Agency Didn't Tell You

"I can't shake the feeling that something is off." "I'm not getting the results I expected." As a digital marketing consultant with decades of experience, I hear these phrases all the time in my initial chats with business owners who are partnered up with a digital marketing agency. Alarm bells go off.

It's not that these agencies are intentionally or maliciously misleading their clients. In fact, sometimes the agency doesn't even realize what it's doing. However, when a key stakeholder reaches out to me with concerns, I'm usually able to trace it back to one of the following "secrets" the agency is keeping.

They Don't Do It All, Let Alone Understand It All

There are presently more than 6,000 digital advertising agencies in the U.S. alone[i]. The figure represents 12 percent year-on-year growth or the addition of more than 600 agencies every year!. So, where do they come from?

Agency owners are usually marketing professionals who previously worked in a specific subset of digital marketing and branched out independently. While that means they have some marketing experience and can speak the language, they don't necessarily understand all aspects of digital marketing or how to ensure you're getting the most from tasks outside their area of expertise.

Let's say your agency's owner has a background in social media marketing. What happens when that person is also tasked with your Pay-Per-Click (PPC) ads or Search Engine Optimization (SEO)?

You won't necessarily get the results you need in those areas, and your agency may not even realize your campaigns are underperforming, let alone why or how to correct them.

There Are Layers Between You and the People Performing Your Marketing Tasks

You may only interface with the agency owner if you're working with a small agency. As agencies grow, they bring on account managers to interact with their customers, and that person will usually be your main point of contact. In either case, you're generally removed from the person completing your digital marketing tasks.

That means when you provide feedback, it passes through several people before the person completing the work hears it. It's like a game of telephone, with no telling what message that person hears. The reverse is also true. It's difficult for professionals to find out details they need, such as information about your branding, customers, and how you operate.

Without direct two-way communication between the company and the digital marketing professional completing the work, brands often come across as less authentic, and businesses get less return on investment.

Some of Your Work is Going to Subcontractors

If internal layers inside a digital marketing agency aren't difficult enough to contend with, agencies often outsource work further to subcontractors, and, no, they won't always tell you they're doing this. That makes it even more challenging to communicate with prospective customers authentically and also means your company's proprietary information is likely being shared with third parties you know nothing about.

There Aren't Any Guarantees

If your digital marketing agency promised they'd get you in the first position on Google, assured you that you'd get a specific number of leads, or vowed to increase your revenue by a certain percentage, you have cause to be wary. There are too many variables to give these kinds of guarantees.

For example, Google changes its algorithm hundreds of times per year. Even if your digital marketing agency is well versed in SEO, you'll occasionally see some shifts as the algorithm changes. The activities of your competitors will impact your marketing results too. This is often seen with PPC ads when competing companies start running ads with keywords already in use by a brand. Sometimes top ranking is achieved with bigger budgets or better-quality content.

They're Either Constantly Pivoting or Should Be

Because results can't be guaranteed, and what gets results will change over time, seasoned digital marketing professionals are diligent and ready to pivot. They're watching performance metrics, running tests to see if results can be improved, and adapting the strategy over time.

If you're not hearing what's changing in your strategy regularly, one of two things is happening. Either they're not changing anything, which means you're not going to improve your results, or they're simply not telling you what they're doing. The latter may be because they're afraid you'll see their pivots as a failure when really, they're an integral part of digital marketing, or it might be because they don't see themselves as your partner.

You Deserve Transparency

Sometimes even agencies that are really good at what they do worry their clients will make changes that will negatively affect campaigns, so they keep essential information under lock and key. However, something is amiss when an agency refuses to let you see what's happening in the background and won't grant access to view your channels or their data.

As a business owner or stakeholder, you should be looped in on what's happening with your digital marketing. That includes things like the pivots mentioned above and key metrics. It also means you should have access to your properties, such as your website, analytics, and social media profiles.

Digital Marketing is a Group Effort

Your business, finance, sales, marketing, and often product development teams need to be connected, and everyone must work together to create transformative results. For example:

Business leaders should be setting the overall company goals and vision, while marketing efforts should be in support of the objectives set.

The marketing department requires a budget but won't likely have adequate funding if the finance department doesn't understand what they're doing or how the marketing investment benefits the brand.

Product developers understand the key points and benefits. They can also convey them to marketing, but marketing will have insights into what customers are looking for and whether product development is meeting their needs.

The marketing team can do much to automate and send better leads to the sales team over time, but hearing feedback from sales on how processes are performing and what leads are saying in one-on-one discussions is invaluable.

The list goes on. This is arguably one of the biggest reasons digital marketing agencies fall short. They work in silos and are removed from your company, making it impossible to create real synergy and get results that impact the company as a whole.

[i] IBISWorld. "Digital Advertising Agencies in the US." IBISWorld.com. https://bit.ly/dmo-2-i

Chapter 3

Best Practices for Finding, Hiring, and Managing Freelancers

Unlike agencies, which don't always offer expertise and create silos, freelancers are often experts in their chosen field and can become an integral part of your team. I routinely bring freelancers in to round out in-house talent in my work as a digital marketing consultant for this reason.

However, there is a learning curve when it comes to finding, hiring, and managing freelancers. I've worked with hundreds on various projects over the years and teach my clients how to find the best talent for their needs. This chapter will help shorten your learning curve.

What to Know Before Hiring a Freelancer

Before I dig into the entire process of finding, hiring, and managing freelancers, I want to address a few points that will help you have more success.

Freelancers are not employees.

It's important to remember that when you hire a freelancer, you're hiring someone to produce something specific or deliver a certain result. You don't necessarily have control over things like how they do it, what tools they use, or when they work.

For example, you can hire a freelancer to do your Facebook marketing, but you can't tell the person they need to attend your daily employee huddle or log in at 8 am to look for replies.

Depending on your jurisdiction, failure to honor the differences can cause legal and tax issues.

You *can* hire a freelancer to fill most digital marketing roles, but that doesn't mean you *should*.

A few digital marketing tasks you can outsource to freelancers include:

- Video Production
- Pay-Per-Click (PPC) Campaign Setup & Management
- Development and Design
- Search Engine Optimization (SEO)
- Analytics
- Social Media Marketing
- Email Marketing
- Copywriting
- Graphic Design and Creative Work
- Digital Marketing Management

With that said, sometimes hiring a freelancer isn't a good idea. For example, the person managing your social media needs to have a pulse on your company's daily activities and be incredibly tuned into your brand. Unfortunately, that's not always possible when the person is removed from your company. The same is true of the person managing your overall digital marketing strategies. Consider the role you need to fill before searching for a freelancer and keep it in-house when it makes more sense to do so.

You must be familiar with the role before you begin.

One of the biggest catch-22s of hiring freelancers is that you need to have at least some background in the role you're filling. This includes the challenges your freelancer may face, potential solutions, tools, industry standards, and how long it typically takes to complete certain projects or tasks. You may want to spend some time looking at freelancers with a wide range of backgrounds and from a range of industries to get a better feel for what's out there and what to expect before you start the recruitment process.

You should know what you want before you try to hire anyone.

Before you put a job post out there or start contacting freelancers, spend some time getting to know what you like. It's helpful to gather samples you like in advance.

For example, if you're hiring a freelancer to design your new website, it's a good idea to find a handful of websites that are similar to what you want and make a note of what it is that you specifically like about them. In this case, you might also want to consider things like SEO, analytics, long-term maintenance, and how your lead generation forms should work.

You need to have a workflow and process in mind.

The processes you set for your first freelancer will likely be the ones you use as you grow. So, although you may be able to "wing it," send things back-and-forth via email, and have a very informal working relationship to start, it's not sustainable as you scale and often sets the stage for miscommunication. A few things to decide before hiring a freelancer include:

- How Projects Will Be Managed/ What Project Management Tool You'll Use
- Deliverables
- Schedule for Deliverables
- When and How Payment Will Be Made
- Project Budgets
- How Edits/ Revisions/ Reworks Will Be Handled

- KPIs for Successful Completion
- Ideal Length of Relationship
- Who Will Own the Rights to the Work

How to Find Freelancers

There are many places to find freelancers. Although it's technically possible to find suitable freelancers on any of them, success rates dramatically increase when you stick to tried-and-true methods.

Freelancer platforms are an excellent place to start.

Freelancer platforms like Upwork and Fiverr can be a great starting point if you've never hired a freelancer before since they make it easy to vet candidates, simplify payments, and offer a layer of protection. For example, many of these platforms will support you if a freelance developer from their site tries to hijack your website. They can withhold payment if your freelance writer submits plagiarized work as well.

In these cases, you can also gauge which freelancers have the most experience. It's advantageous to hire a seasoned freelancer with a proven track record on your initial projects because they'll generally be a bit more stable as you get more experience with freelancer management. It can also help you anticipate what to expect as you add to your expanded team.

Personal recommendations are often safe bets.

If you have a friend or associate in a similar industry who consistently puts out great digital marketing content, ask them if they'll share the name of their freelancer. If you're a member of professional organizations or online groups, you can also put out the word that you're looking for a freelancer. More than one-third of the workforce now freelances[i], but not everyone does it full-time. For this reason, references from others, especially via sites like LinkedIn, can help you find hidden and untapped talent. Bear in mind, however, that you won't have the same tools and resources available that you would with a dedicated platform.

Use caution with classified ad websites and job boards.

You may also find success with job boards and classified sites like Craigslist. But, because the professionals you find through them do not come with any kind of recommendation or protection afforded by other platforms, it can be risky.

Be mindful of "suppliers," "providers," and "mills."

A new breed of website has emerged in recent years that's more like a content marketplace. Instead of hiring a writer or designer directly, you'll usually contract with the company that owns the website and place orders directly through them, be it content marketing materials such as a graphic, blog, or batch of social media posts. The company then farms the work out either directly to a creative or has multiple creatives complete the same project, then lets you choose which you prefer. It can seem like a good deal on the surface, but these outlets don't necessarily attract the best freelance talent, pad prices, and add barriers between you and the person completing your work.

How to Hire Digital Marketing Professionals

At this point, you have a clear idea of what you need from your digital marketing freelancer, know how you'd like to work with them, and have scoped out one or more talent pools. It's time to hire!

Step 1: Write an effective digital marketing job post.

Look at other job posts to get inspiration for yours. As you draft your job description, include the points covered earlier in the workflow section. You may also ask applicants to answer questions as part of the process. You can use the following questions as-is or develop your own from them.

- Which of your previous projects is this one most like and why?
- What's the most difficult freelance project you've accepted, and how did you overcome the challenges?
- What makes you uniquely suited for this project?
- What part of this project excites you most?

Step 2: Check into candidates.

It's tough to know what you should check when hiring a digital marketing freelancer if you haven't hired before, but it's a bit easier if you're working with a dedicated freelancer platform. You can scope out candidates on your own and ask them to apply or simply post your job and examine applications as they roll in. A few things to consider include:

- Good reputation or rating on the platform from previous clients.
- A high number of repeat clients and/or long-term contracts.
- Portfolio of work similar to what you'd like to complete.
- Previous and recent experience working as a freelancer.
- Evidence of skill and/or aptitude tests in the specialty.
- Comfort with the collaboration and project management tools you plan to use.
- Requested wages in line with your expectations and budget.

When interviewing, look for soft skills, such as whether the person asks you questions, communicates well, appears enthusiastic, and if they followed your instructions well.

Step 3: Shortlist your preferred candidates.

Keep a running list of your top candidates as you go. It may help to keep a spreadsheet with profile links and notes about what you liked about a particular candidate.

Step 4: Do a dry run or paid test.

If possible, do a dry run or paid test with your shortlisted candidates. For example, you may want to hire several freelance writers to create the same blog, so it's easier for you to gauge which candidate produces work that most closely matches your goals. With more intensive projects, such as video production, start with a single video.

If you're hiring someone for a longer project, you may want to limit the test period to a week or two. You can also try breaking the first project into milestones with specific deliverables to help ensure things are on the right track.

Although it may not need to be said, do not ask freelancers for unpaid tests or free work. It's typically against the rules of freelancer platforms and is poor etiquette that can end relationships with seasoned freelancers before they even start.

Step 5: Provide meaningful feedback.

Spend time reviewing your freelancer's work when it's submitted. Let them know what you liked about it and also what they could have done, if anything, to produce something more in line with your goals.

At this point, you may already have your dream freelance digital marketing professional. Congratulations! Or, if you're extra lucky and can't decide which freelancer is best, do a second dry run or hire them both and alternate between them. Good help is hard to find!

Don't forget to let anyone who didn't make the cut know. If you wish, you can tell them why you went with another candidate, ask them if it's ok to contact them later if things don't work out (if you mean it), or, at the very least, formally end the contract if you're working through a freelancer platform.

How to Keep Working with a Good Digital Marketing Freelancer

More than 30 percent of Fortune 500 companies and up to 70 percent of small businesses work with freelancers[ii]. That means there are plenty of opportunities for a good freelancer to find other work if things don't pan out with you.

When you find a freelancer you like working with, let them know. To maintain a healthy long-term relationship, it's also a good idea to:

- Give them positive feedback first every time, especially if you're pairing it with constructive feedback.
- Be organized.
- Thank them for their hard work.
- Pay them fairly, fully, and on time.
- Be responsive to their needs and questions.
- Leave positive reviews or recommendations for them.
- Send potential clients their way.
- Offer them first choice on any projects you start and/or additional work.
- Step back and give them room to work.

Building a digital marketing dream team takes time. By following the steps outlined here, you can streamline the process and retain talent longer, so your results continue to improve over time, and you can maintain focus on your business.

 [i] Edelman Intelligence/ Upwork Inc. "Freelance Forward." Upwork.com. https://bit.ly/dmo-3-i

 [ii] Elsie Boskamp. "43 Profound Freelance Statistics: Facts, Trends, Predictions." Zippia.com. https://bit.ly/dmo-3-ii

Chapter 4

The Cost of Outsourcing Digital Marketing Activities

Questions about cost inevitably come up when people begin to explore the viability of digital marketing outsourcing. As an experienced digital marketing consultant with a business background, I can certainly provide some insight.

Before I start breaking things down, though, let me ask you this: *How much does it cost to build a house?*

You probably have lots of questions for me now. *How big is the house? What types of materials? How will the space be used, and what amenities does it need to have?*

A modest tiny house can now be built for a few thousand dollars, but a luxurious mansion will set someone back millions. This is the case with calculating the cost of outsourcing digital marketing too.

You can hire and manage a freelancer on a per-project basis and perhaps pay less than $100 for that single project, or you can spend millions on the strategy and management of all your digital marketing activities. Neither of these extremes is likely right for your business—especially if you operate a small business.

The question, then, isn't "How much does outsourcing digital marketing cost?" Instead, it should be something more along the lines of, "What's the right digital marketing investment based on my business's current status and goals?" But, of course, the answer will be different for everyone reading this.

With that in mind, this chapter will break down some of the most common digital marketing outsourcing costs and provide a basic framework for calculating the right investment for your business.

The Cost of Outsourcing Digital Marketing vs Managing it In-House

Outsourcing is often a popular choice because it's cheaper. For example, wage and salary costs account for around 71 percent of a typical employee's compensation, according to the Bureau of Labor Statistics (BLS)[i]. The remaining 29 percent of compensation is put toward employee benefits. When you outsource, the latter is an expense your business does not have to shoulder, so you see an immediate savings of nearly 30 percent there. When talent is carefully sourced, businesses will see gains from improved efficiency and improved ROI too.

The Cost of Outsourcing Digital Marketing Activities

Digital marketing is a broad term that can relate to a variety of activities such as:

- Development
- Search Engine Optimization (SEO)
- Pay-Per-Click (PPC) Ads
- Video Production
- Email Marketing
- Copywriting
- Social Media Marketing
- Graphic Design
- Analytics
- Management

Some components require greater in-depth knowledge and take more time than others. A solid digital marketing strategy will generally touch on all these areas and more, but if you're a small business owner trying to manage it on your own, you might only start with one or two areas. Don't worry if you don't know where to begin yet. You'll learn how to create your roadmap in the next chapter. For now, let's just focus on investments.

Development: $1,000 to $300,000+ one time plus upkeep.

Development relates to creating a website or application for your business. If you want a very basic template-built website, you might be able to find someone who will do it for around $1,000. The site may feature your logo and brand colors, but it probably won't be tailored to your visitors or optimized for search engines. It also won't likely integrate with your CRM or have special features such as product guides and listings. As spend increases, you transition from having a nice-looking website to a website that attracts and converts leads, plus automates processes to save you money over time.

Search Engine Optimization: $1,000 to $30,000 per month.

SEO involves a lot of tasks and skills ranging from keyword research to technical on-site optimization, linking strategies, content marketing, and analytics. While it's possible to find someone who will carry out specific SEO tasks at an hourly rate, most SEO agencies require a monthly retainer in the neighborhood of $1,000 to $2,000 to start. Expect to pay more if you're in a in a competitive niche.

Pay-Per-Click Ad Management: $1,000 to $8,000+ Per Month

Calculating the cost of pay-per-click ads is a bit trickier because there are many different pricing structures and costs involved. Agencies won't typically take on projects unless the raw monthly ad spend is at least a few thousand dollars, with some requiring a minimum spend of $10,000 or more. The cost to manage it is a separate charge and usually managed as a monthly retainer either at a flat rate or a percentage of your ad spend. Something in the realm of ten to 15 percent is normal. That means if you're spending $10,000 on ads monthly, the management will be an additional $1,000 to $1,500. However, some larger PPC agencies are compensated by the advertising platforms (such as Google Ads or Bing Ads), which saves you the cost of paying a separate management fee.

A good PPC manager will work hard, always monitoring the results and testing different keywords, ad copy, and landing pages. As a result, your ROI will get better over time. The challenge is that many use a "set it and forget it" mentality.

Video Production: $2,000 to $20,000+ per video.

Video is another area with massive variances. Let's say you want a basic one or two-minute animated explainer that requires a script, uses stock animation, and has a professional voice actor. The starting point for outsourcing video production will be around $2,000. The price will increase if you want custom characters, specialized animation, need a longer video, and so forth.

Sometimes businesses want actual footage of their employees, locations, and customers. It's more intensive because there's a camera crew, setup, more editing, and other expenses involved. Expect a project like this to start at around $7,000, with $10,000 to $15,000 being a more likely sweet spot for professional video production.

Email Marketing: $500 to $2,000+ per month.

If you're outsourcing email marketing to a top-rated freelancer, you're likely to pay between $60 and $150 per hour. In this sense, you can somewhat customize the level of service you receive. For example, you may simply have your freelancer design and write your campaigns while you manage your segmentation and other concerns. Agencies, on the other hand, often work with retainers or packages. So, for example, you might get a single email per month for $500 or three for $1,500.

It's important to note that there are other costs involved. For example, your email service provider may charge for each email you send or have a monthly fee based on total contacts. With this in mind, it's ill-advised to hire someone who simply writes and designs emails. You need someone keeping your lists clean and monitoring for issues to ensure messages don't start going to spam. There's a fair amount of setup and "seeding" when you first begin mailing or using a new email address too. Furthermore, your email marketing professional needs to constantly test different techniques and monitor analytics to ensure you're improving results and ROI over time.

Copywriting: $200 to $3,000+ per month.

Sorting out the cost of outsourcing copywriting is enough to make anyone's head spin. Depending on the arrangement, you can pay by word, per hour, per piece, or for blocks of content. If you're purchasing unedited work from a general copywriter, expect the starting rate to be around $100 per 1,000-word blog. If you're working with a specialty writer who knows your niche, you'll pay 25-50 percent more. Agencies and copywriting firms sometimes have editors who can help with strategy and finding the right copywriter. Still, you'll generally pay three or four times the amount you might have without the extra overhead.

Of course, a single blog per month isn't likely to get you the traffic you want. Two is a better starting point, though you may need more if you're in a competitive niche and trying to gain ground. You may also need your copywriter to help with web pages, whitepapers, and other types of content.

Social Media Marketing: $900 to $20,000 per month.

Before we dig into investments, it's important to note that social media marketing, management, and advertising are three different things.

- *A social media manager* behaves as if they are your brand online. They'll engage with people, respond to comments, post, and ensure that profile information is updated.

- *A social media marketer* is strategic. They'll devise campaigns designed to grow your audience and engage readers with the ultimate goal of encouraging people to visit your website or become leads.
- *A social media advertising specialist* is focused on paid ads and posts. The role is similar to a PPC specialist in which lead generation is the ultimate goal, though the individual is more familiar with the nuances of each social platform.

Sometimes professionals cover all three areas, but it's often just one or two. Whereas a freelancer may work by the hour, and the total cost will vary based on the number of networks, total posts, and similar factors, agencies usually work with a flat rate that starts at around $1,000 per month—the cost of ads and things like contests to grow your audience increases the amount from there.

Graphic Design: $25 to $60 per hour.

If your outsourced graphic designer is working full-time hours for your company, costs can easily exceed $5,000 per month and approach $10,000.

This is generally overkill for small businesses, though. You may only tag a graphic designer in to help with special projects, such as designing whitepapers, case studies, and infographics, in which case your costs will likely be under $1,000 per month. However, many businesses also have their designer help with images for social media and similar recurring needs, which may double or triple the amount.

Analytics: $1,000 to $2,000 per month.

The challenge with analytics is twofold. First, you need to have the right tools to collect and present relevant data to your analytics professional. Some tools are free, but you can easily spend $1,000 or more on a single tool as you move into more advanced marketing. Then, you need the analytics professional to turn that data into results your team can actually use to improve the effectiveness and ROI of your marketing. It's easy to see how large companies with many working gears can spend tens of thousands each month on analytics. However, a growth-minded small business should plan for at least $1,000 per month if outsourcing.

Management: $6,000 to $40,000+ per month.

A digital marketing manager oversees all the processes outlined above. In a very small company, the manager may perform some of the marketing tasks. However, the role generally relates more toward ensuring all campaigns are performing, the team is working in tandem, deadlines are being met, and goals are hit.

The Cost of Outsourcing Digital Marketing to Freelancers vs an Agency vs a Consultant

As you may have noticed in the examples above, working with agencies or marketing firms is usually two to three times more than hiring a freelancer directly. However, when you hire freelance marketers, you then become responsible for finding and managing them. Therefore, a third option is to work with a digital marketing consultant who will find the best solution for each marketing role for your business.

Calculating the Total Cost of Outsourcing Digital Marketing Activities

If you were adding things up as we went, you might have noticed the minimum cost to outsource digital marketing comes to around $10,000. However, this is not necessarily going to be your cost. Remember, in the beginning, I asked you to rephrase your question and think of it as "What's the right digital marketing investment based on my business's current status and goals?"

If you're focused on fast sales, invest $10,000 in a month, and net $20,000, that was money well spent. Equally, if each of your sales becomes a contract worth a million dollars, it might make sense for you to invest $100,000 or more each month even if you don't close a single sale to start.

It's not necessarily about what you spend. It's about getting the return on investment. With that in mind, I advocate for putting an expert at the helm of each of your digital marketing activities and working your way through the various activities at scale.

[i] U.S. Department of Labor, Bureau of Labor Statistics. "Employer Costs for Employee Compensation." BLS.gov. https://bit.ly/dmo-4-1

Chapter 5

Climbing the Digital Marketing Tree

O ptions to promote your business online are seemingly endless. It's impossible to start with them all at once, and even if you could, most businesses would spread their resources too thin to find success with any one of them. Being strategic is essential. You should be familiar with all the marketing channels available to your business and how those channels and their strategies intersect with one another and increase your reach far beyond what traditional marketing can do.

I like to use the analogy of the digital marketing tree to simplify these concepts. If you picture a fruit tree, you'll likely see some fruit on the ground, more on the lower branches, some you can reach if you stretch, and some near the top that will take you a bit of time and effort to get to.

It's the same in digital marketing. I refer to these groups as ground fruit, low-hanging fruit, mid-range fruit, and distant fruit and place different marketing activities in each. That way, it's easy to see what to prioritize and why as you plan your next steps.

Ground Fruit

Gather the ground fruit first. It's the easiest to collect. Plus, ground fruit activities often fuel your future digital marketing activities and they, in turn, will improve the results you get from your ground fruit activities too. Your business website and email marketing are good examples.

Everything leads back to your website.

Virtually every activity you undertake, whether the goal is conversions, brand awareness, or lead generation, will involve directing people to your website as you move forward. It's the foundation for every other element of your strategy, so you want to start here first.

Email marketing should be an early activity too.

The barrier to entry for email marketing is low,

and it requires one of the lowest investments overall. Email marketing delivers an average of $36 ROI for every $1 spent[i], so it's something you'll want to consider right away. With email marketing, you can easily use lists to categorize current and potential customers and keep driving them back to your website. Newsletters work similarly, though typically have the goal of re-engagement and driving people back to your site for more information.

Low-Hanging Fruit

Low-hanging fruit represents opportunities to create a large impact with a minimal investment. Social media marketing and paid search fit into this category. You'll want to work on them after you feel confident with your ground fruit initiatives.

Social media is effective when you have a solid strategy.

Choosing one or two social media platforms to focus on and establishing your online networks is a low-cost, high-reward technique. Platforms such as Twitter, Facebook, Instagram, LinkedIn, Pinterest, and YouTube present perfect opportunities to reach potential customers and increase brand awareness. Sharing updates and fresh, high-quality content regularly on a handful of platforms will give you a strong presence without demanding a large investment. An effective social media strategy can take several months of continuous effort before you see a significant payoff.

Paid ads complement an organic strategy.

Paid search is a guaranteed way to start driving traffic immediately to your website and achieve results faster than organic strategies. Moreover, using paid ads (pay-per-click or PPC) and content marketing together will simultaneously allow your content to reach new people while cultivating existing relationships. Once you've decided to invest in a search campaign or social ad campaign, your digital advertising campaigns will require ongoing changes and constant monitoring to make sure that they produce desired results.

Mid-Range Fruit

Mid-range digital fruits require comparatively larger resource investments to develop, plan, and implement than the aforementioned low-hanging fruit, so they're best left until your earlier initiatives are implemented. Search engine optimization (SEO) and content marketing fit within this category.

SEO will give your brand a major advantage but takes time to deliver results.

Unlike paid search, SEO is more complex and takes longer to deliver results. With that being said, having a high organic ranking for industry terms is a huge advantage to have over your competitors. Taking SEO into consideration early is a smart choice as it takes time to build enough content, optimized web pages, and referral links to achieve strong search rankings.

Content marketing builds relationships that turn into sales.

Content marketing is more time-consuming than creating simple social media content. Detailed pieces of content such as blog posts or articles, infographics, e-books, videos, and how-to guides require a bit more research and time to prepare. While the content of this nature takes time to create, its impact and value are significant. These elements help establish your organization as an industry leader and get people interested in coming back for information.

Distant Fruit

Toward the top of the tree, you have the digital fruit that takes the most time and planning to leverage. Analytics and mobile strategies fit into this category.

Analytics will help you improve your strategies and improve ROI.

Analytics is an element that can be included in every other digital marketing strategy. From simple analytic points such as social media engagement to tracking paid search conversions, analytics lets you determine whether you are achieving your goals with the digital marketing efforts you're dedicating to various marketing channels and increasing your ROI.

Mobile initiatives can be beneficial with certain audiences.

Components for mobile devices are also technical in nature and more difficult to implement. Consider Apps, QR codes, and local search as avenues for promoting your brand among mobile users.

Climb Strategically

If you haven't started leveraging any digital marketing strategies yet, use the digital marketing tree as your roadmap, so each effort builds on those that came before it. It's ok if you've already started in a different order too. However, you will improve your results if you refocus your efforts lower down the tree as you move forward.

[i] Megan Moller. "The ROI of Email Marketing [Infographic]." Litmus. https://bit.ly/dmo-5-1

Chapter 6

Should You Outsource Digital Marketing Management or Keep it In-House?

At this point, you should have a firm understanding of the different types of digital marketing available, what to focus on first, and enough background on outsourcing to have an idea of what it can do for you and your business. Now, it's time to start making some decisions about how to structure your outsourcing strategy in a way that aligns with business operations and goals.

Strong digital marketing management is the cornerstone of all online marketing efforts and plays a crucial role in the overall growth of an organization. Particularly now, with marketing spend on the rise, it's essential for organizations to ensure this vital role is being fulfilled by the right person with the right expertise. That means you'll want to fill the role first if you're serious about achieving your business goals through digital marketing initiatives.

You'll also want to review the role and your options, even if you already have someone in place. You may not need to outsource the position in the end, but understanding it will help you ensure whoever is responsible is performing in a way that takes your digital marketing in the direction it needs to go.

The Role of a Digital Marketing Manager

A digital marketing manager blends business prowess with creativity while overseeing all your digital channels and managing the team responsible for producing marketing materials.

This includes things like written content, social media, email marketing, SEO, and online advertising. They craft campaigns around business goals, observe the latest trends, monitor analytics, and adjust the strategy as needed to improve results.

The role is unique because a digital marketing manager needs to be an expert in all digital marketing activities to troubleshoot issues and help the digital marketing team hone their skills.

Core Competencies and Resources

The first thing to consider when filling the role of a marketing manager is whether it's possible for someone on your in-house team to have all the competencies and resources necessary to do the job well. If you already have someone on your team performing the job, don't evaluate the person in the role now. Only consider competencies and resources as they relate to the role as a whole.

A good digital marketing manager will have a diverse skill set.

Skills to look for include:

- An understanding of your brand
- An understanding of your niche market and audience(s)
- An understanding of the company's objectives
- Data analysis
- Comfort with AI and automation
- Communication
- Leadership

Marketing managers should know how to work with various tools.

Some of the most common tools leveraged include:

- Analytics
- Social media marketing
- Customer relationship management (CRM) systems
- Content management systems (CMS)
- Search Engine Optimization (SEO)
- Content creation- graphics, word processing and editing, video

- Email marketing
- Collaboration

A marketing manager must have enough time to devote to the job.

Many growing businesses have a "marketing manager," but the person is also the business owner, works in an administrative role, or has other duties within the company. These setups don't generally provide an employee with enough time to devote to marketing and produce measurable results. Research shows only 14 percent of digital marketers work part-time and nearly half put in at least nine hours per day[i], so this is a role that typically receives full-time attention and then some.

However, it's important to note that the number of hours invested doesn't always correlate with results. For example, a digital marketing manager may invest more time while getting the team up and running or while organizing a campaign. Equally, they may require less time once processes are in place and when campaigns are performing well.

Identifying Success in Digital Marketing Management

Simply put, the key performance indicators (KPIs) to measure the success of your digital marketing manager will be the same KPIs you're using to measure the individual campaigns and processes across all your digital marketing efforts. The metrics you use may change based on the campaigns being run and your corporate objectives.

Use KPIs to measure success.

We'll dig deeper into key marketing metrics in a later chapter. However, a few things to consider for this role include:

- Sales revenue generated by marketing
- Return on marketing investment (ROMI)
- Cost per lead
- Customer lifetime value
- Traffic-to-lead ratio
- Lead progress ratios
- Landing page conversion rates
- Organic traffic
- Social media metrics
- Inbound link performance
- Mobile data

Making the Final Decision

Finding a digital marketing manager with the skills to drive your organization forward isn't easy. It may be tempting to outsource to a third party with a demonstrated track record across multiple companies.

The challenge here is that this role isn't only about skill. Your digital marketing manager needs to know your company; the brand, objectives, customers, and more. If they don't have a pulse on the day-to-day happenings of the company, it will be impossible to ensure the digital marketing strategy is in alignment with the organization.

With that in mind, you can outsource digital marketing management, but the person responsible for fulfilling the role needs to become part of the team. This is similar to how I work as a consultant. Although I'm not an employee of the companies I serve, I learn everything I can about them and connect with the leadership team before suggesting any strategic measures.

I'm also very hands-on, interacting with all departments to bring strategies into alignment, and am engaged on a daily basis. If you can create a similar arrangement with your digital marketing manager, outsourcing may work well for you. If not, it's best to keep this as an in-house role.

[i] Angel Niñofranco. "How Many Hours Do Digital Marketers Work Per Day? [POLL]." Search Engine Journal. https://bit.ly/dmo-6-i

Chapter 7

Content Marketing Calendar: What it is and Why You Need One

Content marketing calendars are good practice in general, but they become indispensable when you're outsourcing. Though they don't take much time or cost a lot of money to make, they radically change how the team operates and can dramatically improve results. You'll want to ensure you have one or your digital marketing manager is creating and maintaining one as you kick things off.

How Content Marketing Calendars Work?

There are many different types of calendars your marketing team may use. A digital marketing calendar, for example, outlines all your marketing initiatives. There are also editorial calendars, which are more of a high-level overview of the themes and topics an organization plans to cover over an extended period. Many teams will develop an editorial calendar a full year in advance or even use the same editorial calendar template year after year. A content calendar, on the other hand, focuses solely on the content aspect of your marketing strategy. Think of it as a creation and publishing schedule for all the pieces of content your marketing team generates or a detailed document that guides the daily activities of informed marketers.

What this looks like in action may vary somewhat within each organization, but let's say you run a travel company. Your editorial calendar might say you plan to cover romantic getaways in January to get a head start on Valentine's Day, then tropical destinations the next month, spring break trips the following month, and so forth.

Then, your content calendar for January will list specific blogs on the topic of romantic getaways your team will release, such as international destinations for couples, Valentine's staycations, and so forth. You'll also outline corresponding social posts, your digital newsletter topics, and any other content to be shared during that period.

As a final layer, you'll have the full digital marketing calendar. It will include other aspects we visited on the digital marketing tree, such as website refreshes, SEO initiatives, and PPC ads. Some may not relate to your editorial or content calendar, but often it makes more sense to have a cohesive approach. For example, suppose you're running with a romantic getaways theme in January, and you have excellent content releasing related to the theme. In that case, it makes sense to work on related SEO keywords simultaneously and run ads that cover the theme. You'll get more mileage from your efforts and better results that way, but of course, it all comes back to having a solid content calendar first.

How Content Calendars Improve Your Outsourcing Results

As you can see, a good content calendar is the central component of a high-quality content strategy. This is true regardless of whether you outsource. However, when companies outsource, two new challenges emerge. First, the marketing team grows rapidly. Leadership teams need methods to keep everyone and everything organized. Second, the team is likely split in many ways. They're working remotely on different schedules and likely working without much direct or one-to-one contact. You can't just stop by someone's desk to touch base. You need a governing document that clarifies who's responsible for what.

Content calendars help you think more critically about goals and resources.

Writing blog posts for visibility and brand awareness? Research shows you should be writing one to four posts per week[i]. Writing them for SEO value? That's three to five.

If you're leveraging social media marketing, each platform has specific guidelines for frequency. LinkedIn, for example, tends to do best with five posts per week, no more than once per day[ii]. Facebook is roughly the same, and Twitter essentially needs as many posts as you can muster. Guidelines for platforms like YouTube, Instagram, and Pinterest vary because it takes time to create high-quality content. It's better to put out a single top-tier video each month than it is to release four low-quality ones.

Then, there are marketing emails and email newsletters. Nearly 90 percent of your customers want to hear from you at least monthly, and just over 60 percent say at least weekly[iii]. If you exceed their optimal number of sends, you run the risk of getting unsubscribes, so it's generally best to stop there unless you have something incredibly important to convey.

Exhausted already? We haven't even gotten into the best times to post and all the other mediums you could potentially be using in your content marketing plan. But, consistency is key to maintaining engagement and ensuring your content marketing efforts produce results.

When you outline all the content types you need in advance, it's much easier to determine how to allocate resources, get it on your team's schedules, and ensure all related components are completed on time so they can be released together. Without this crucial resource, it's very easy to lose track of content ideas or forget to save enough time for content creation.

All your marketing campaigns can feed into one another.

It's often said that people need to hear something seven times before they retain it. That might not be a proven fact, but we know repetition is essential for memory recall, and your prospects are being hit with an endless stream of information all day, every day. With that in mind, you need to ensure your messaging is consistent and use the same messaging repeatedly. Your content calendar will help you do just this.

The other big thing is that it's much easier to create several pieces of related content at once than it is to come back to an idea later. You shouldn't be writing a single blog on a topic and then move on. The details of that blog can be converted into social posts, emails, and even a video. When you work in groups like this, you'll be more efficient. Plus, your audience will naturally hear the same core concepts, and they'll have access to your expert content on whichever medium suits them.

To make your content go even further, do some keyword research and highlight which keywords you plan to cover on your content calendar too. This way, you'll naturally build strong SEO across a wide variety of topics that relate to your business.

Ownership of duties is clear.

Once your content strategy is up and running and your team is accustomed to working together, it will be like a fine-tuned machine. However, in the early days of outsourcing, it's common to have some uncertainty over who is creating which piece of content or where one job ends and the next one starts. A good content calendar outlines all the jobs and who's responsible for what. This eliminates confusion. It can go a long way to ensuring you have the right resources and that each person has enough time for their individual tasks too.

Deadlines are more easily met.

Most growth-minded businesses have several people working on content at once. For example, suppose you're releasing a single blog. In that case, you'll have one person identifying which keywords to use, a writer, perhaps a graphic designer, an editor or manager, and possibly others reviewing the content for accuracy and tone. Each person needs to stay on track. A content calendar helps immensely with this and lets the team see the bigger picture, which can also boost adherence to deadlines.

You can track your marketing budget and results better.

Small businesses reinvest around eight percent of their annual revenue into marketing[iv]. It's a small amount, so it's important to make every dollar count. First, find out how much it costs to make different content types and track that alongside your projects on your calendar. Then, watch your engagements, leads, and conversions to see which types of content and which topics perform best. From there, you can turn up the volume on the things that are working and let go of the things that aren't to get more return from your marketing budget over time.

Best Practices for Using a Content Calendar Effectively

Now that you understand the basics of content calendars and how they help, let's explore a few things you or your digital marketing manager can do to use yours more effectively.

Use a content calendar tool.

While you can use a specialized platform or content calendar template, basic spreadsheets in Google Sheets or Excel may be sufficient for smaller marketing teams. Google Calendar works well for some too. Consider how you and your team work best and choose a system that helps you visualize the data in a way that's easy to follow.

Understand the key elements of a content calendar.

No matter which tool you use, all good content marketing calendar templates include the same critical elements.

- **Content Form:** Are you creating a blog, social post, video, infographic, or something else?
- **Channel:** Make note of where the content will be shared.
- **Title or Subject:** A working title is fine to start. You can polish it up when you're creating the content.
- **Keywords:** To get more traffic from your content, it should be keyword optimized. Include keywords in your content calendar

so you can build ideas around them, and your work will read more naturally.

- **Deadlines:** Again, each stage should be clearly mapped out with the name of the person responsible for meeting the deadline.
- **Buyer Persona:** Your content should speak directly to your audience, so include personas in your calendar. This primes the person creating the content and helps ensure you're not overlooking any of your personas in your content strategy.
- **Call-to-Action:** Even if your goal is to engage readers in a non-sales way, you should still leave them with a next step and measure how many people take that step. Make sure to leave a spot for a call-to-action (CTA) on your template.
- **Notes:** If you have ideas you want to include, reference links, inspiration links, or anything else the team needs to know, save space for that too.

Add items to your calendar.

Start with a broad approach and then work your way down to the details. That means you'll need to begin with your objectives and budget, nail down how much content you intend to create and your publishing schedule, build out an editorial calendar or outline of broad topics you want to cover, then start brainstorming content that fits into those buckets.

Schedule every part of the creation process.

Remember, some pieces of content can take weeks or more to create and require coordinating the work of several specialists. Give yourself ample time for the creation process and plan to have the work completed and staged at least a week or two in advance. You may need a separate program, referred to as a project management tool, for this. You'll learn how to choose one in the next chapter.

Perform regular content audits.

During an audit, you'll look through all your organization's content and make notes related to how each one is performing, which persona it's designed for, and what stage of the customer journey it addresses. This simple step will show you what's performing well, so you can duplicate your success, close holes in your content strategy, and provide insights on which pieces you can update, improve, or recycle.

[i] Kayla Carmicheal. "How Often Should You (or Your Company) Blog? [New Data]." HubSpot. https://bit.ly/dmo-7-i

 [ii] Daria Marmer. "How Frequently Should I Publish on Social Media? A HubSpot Experiment." HubSpot. https://bit.ly/dmo-7-ii

 [iii] Daniel Burstein. "Email Research Chart: How often customers want to receive promotional emails." Marketing Sherpa. https://bit.ly/dmo-7-iii

 [iv] Caroline Forsey. "How Much Should Your Marketing Team Budget? [By Industry]." HubSpot. https://bit.ly/dmo-7-iv

Chapter 8

Project Management Platforms

L ike content calendars, project management platforms are valuable for any marketing team. They keep everyone in sync and boost success rates by 426 percent[i]. If you're outsourcing, your project management platform becomes the glue that holds everything together too. Plan on integrating one around the time you bring on a digital marketing manager or procuring one now if you already have someone in place. Your manager will be using the tool all day, every day, so the earlier they start using it, the better.

This chapter will help you select the right project management platform for your needs, though you may also want to bring your digital marketing manager in on the discussion too. An experienced manager will likely have used several and can provide practical insights. Furthermore, allowing them to be part of the discussion can help get their buy-in on the software—something that becomes more important if you've decided to work with existing in-house talent and they're adjusting to rapid changes alongside you.

Why Project Management Software is Essential

Once you see how project management software transforms your daily operations and success, you'll wonder how you ever functioned without it. It will help you:

- Get and stay organized. You'll have a place for everything and know where it is.
- Stay on track. You'll know where you and your team are at any given time and can monitor deadlines easier.

- See the big picture when planning. You'll be able to spot bumps in the road before you hit them.
- Manage resources more effectively. You'll know which team members are at, over, and under capacity at a glance.
- Collaborate easier. Many offer real-time synching of docs and communication tools, so your team works as a cohesive unit without constant email barrages.
- Manage file-sharing better. You can do away with messy DropBox, Google Drive, and OneDrive setups. All files can be kept with their tasks and projects.
- Streamline your workflow. Many programs include time tracking tools, project management, project communication, file sharing, and finance tools, so you can work in one place and often save money by dropping extra tools. Automation is key in this respect too.

What to Look For

Your marketing team doesn't work exactly like the team down the street or even like other teams in your company. It's normal to have some variation, and you should be doing what works best for you. However, to meet the diverse needs of different teams, each platform approaches project management a bit differently and will offer unique tools. A few features to look for include:

- Project overviews. Team members should have some degree of transparency to see how the work they're doing impacts the bigger picture.
- Collaboration tools. Downloading documents and working locally is chaotic for teams. You never know if you've got the most current version or if you're undoing someone else's work. Many tools offer document collaboration and in-task or in-project messaging, so it's easy to find information.
- Real-time updates. You should see changes on documents, notifications, and message boards right away to maximize efficiency.
- Status tracking. Customizable statuses and the ability to filter by status make it easy to

see what people are working on and how close tasks are to being done.

- Review and approval process. Sometimes you can get around having approval tools by using status tracking and team collaboration tools. Still, the process is much more streamlined when stakeholders can provide digital approval rather than writing notes back and forth.
- Customizable workflows. You'll save time and money with customizable workflows, such as automated notifications, reporting, and task generation.
- Customizable views. Everybody works best in a different way. Moreover, how you work best may differ based on the task at hand. Watch for software that offers Gantt charts, timelines, or calendars to give you an overview, as well as Kanban card-style layouts and lists to zero in on specific projects and tasks.
- Reporting. Robust time tracking and project-based analytics will help you manage resources better and identify bottlenecks.
- Integrations and scalability. Choose software that integrates with other platforms and tools. You may not need them right away, but you're likely to find that as you begin to work more fluidly with your new marketing project management

platform, you'll find many ways you can use it to automate and streamline your processes.

Commonly Used Project Management Tools

As a digital marketing consultant, I gravitate to specific platforms as I'm helping teams set up their processes. However, I also recognize that each team and person might use the same software differently. There's no singular best one for that reason.

Details on some of the most common project management tools are outlined below. I encourage you to look at the distinct features offered and compare them to see which ones align with your processes and needs.

Asana

Asana is an excellent project management software tool that often makes it to shortlists. It's one of the few that truly understands that people work differently and offers a multitude of ways to view information and manage work. Whereas virtually all tools offer task management and project management, Asana sets itself apart by providing a level up from this—portfolios. You might use their portfolio management tools if you're coordinating work across several departments within your company, such as product development, sales, and marketing or if you want to divide the work of different specialties, such as video creation, web development/ design, pay-per-click, SEO, social media marketing, and written content. You might use it if you're responsible for overseeing multiple locations or teams too.

That said, it isn't as strong as some of the others in a few areas. It doesn't have a native document editor for streamlined collaboration or the ability to track time, and the reporting tools are a bit lighter than others.

Basecamp

Basecamp is another tool that makes many shortlists. While it offers much in the way of project management, Basecamp sets itself apart in collaboration. For example, it has a messaging app called Campfire, and managers can automate recurring questions for their team. There's also a client view function that makes it easy to share specific details with external stakeholders. That can be especially helpful if you have brand partners, reciprocal referral programs, or you co-market with other companies— perhaps you invite related brands to participate in your webinars, and you want their approval on marketing assets before they go live.

It's also one of the simplest programs, but that comes at a price. It's missing a lot of the bells and whistles others have, and there's little you can do to tailor the software to your needs.

Brightpod

Specifically designed for marketing teams, Brightpod is likely to show up in your searches too. It's user-friendly and offers key functions like tasks, milestones, and workflows. Work is split into pods, and each pod will have its own manager.

However, it is geared more toward marketing agencies. Much of its focus goes to things like time tracking for proper billing of different clients rather than project management features like hierarchical tasks. That means it's not ideal for managing your outsourced digital marketing team, but it's covered here because it's likely to come up in your discussions.

Clarizen

Clarizen is a solid platform that offers a lot of high-level information for an agile project manager. The Exec Dashboard has all sorts of measurements, including cost data, open tickets, a visual product roadmap, project performance, and more.

For that reason, Clarizen is a good enterprise-level solution, but it's not quite as intuitive or user-friendly as some of the others designed for collaboration. It also doesn't offer much in the way of marketing-specific tools and lacks native integrations. Like Brightpod, it's mentioned here because you'll probably see the name elsewhere, but it's one you will likely cross off your list of contenders early.

Filestage

If you have an intensive approval process for marketing materials or you routinely have key stakeholders review content before it's released, Filestage may be the tool you're looking for. It allows you to upload documents and images as well as audio and video files and allows reviewers to annotate the file in a number of ways, so it's easy to see what changes are being requested.

It's excellent in this respect, but you may want to look at other tools if you're looking for software that is more geared toward helping you keep track of your endless task list.

Mavenlink

Another one you're likely to come across is Mavenlink. The platform refers to itself as a project and resource management tool for businesses in the professional services industry, including marketing teams.

With that in mind, it's designed to give a broader perspective on project management and includes things like budgeting features and the ability to share with people outside the team. It lacks some task-specific features that help manage things better at a granular level, but it integrates with other tools like SalesForce and Google Workspace to fill in some of the gaps.

ProofHub

If you're looking for a marketing project management platform that functions more like a virtual office, ProofHub should make your shortlist. The platform lets you visualize your workload in many different ways (table/ task list, Kanban, Gantt, calendar view), plus it allows you to store documents and proof them. There's also chat and announcements, plus the ability to create your own dashboard with a "me-view." Project leaders have solid control over who sees what, plus time tracking, reporting, integration, and more.

The drawback to ProofHub is that payment for this tool is a bit different than others. While most will charge by the user or tier, ProofHub charges by the feature. That means you can get just about anything you want from them and not pay for features you'll never use, but it can also make estimating your costs a bit more challenging, especially if you've never used a project management tool and aren't sure which features your team will actually need and use.

Teamwork Projects

Another solid end-to-end system is Teamwork Projects. It helps you nail the granular details with task management while layering in things like time tracking, resource management, and reporting. It also has portfolio management, which can be beneficial if you're trying to segment marketing based on specialty or asset type.

It's important to note that Teamwork Projects is part of the Teamwork suite. While you can use it alone, you may find that you need to purchase other Teamwork products to get the functionality others provide in their core product, such as chat and content collaboration. However, it also has a CRM and helpdesk platform designed to integrate seamlessly, so it may be a good bet if you plan to grow and don't want to piecemeal products.

Trello

Founded in 2011, Trello is one of the more established platforms on this list. Although the company didn't create Kanban boards, it certainly popularized them. Naturally, that's where the product genuinely shines. Everything you need for a task or project "lives" inside cards. You can assign cards, create lists within cards, attach files, discuss the task or project on the card, and more.

However, Trello stops short of being a comprehensive platform. You can get around things like lack of an approval process by creating lists for each stage of approval or lack of integrated document collaboration by tapping into Google Workspace integration and Google Docs. However, it may not be the solution for you if you're not in love with Kanban or need more reporting tools.

Workamajig

If you like the idea of an all-in-one system, Workamajig might be for you. It includes project management as well as CRM and finance. Although perhaps designed more for agency use, Workamajig's efficiency and reporting tools can help marketing departments maximize their budgets, create streamlined workflows, and improve ROI. Dashboards are customizable by role, and it has robust task management features like proofing and approval.

The company released an updated version a couple of years back that was not received well by users and was arguably buggy. Although the bugs have since largely been squashed, the updated version still has a bit of a learning curve and might not be ideal for those who have not used a project management system before.

Workfront

Originally launched in 2001 under the name AtTask, Workfront is one of the best enterprise project management solutions for marketers. It hits on things others miss, like prioritization, and offers intuitive project dashboards that make it easy to see all project-related data at a glance, down to individual tasks, employees assigned to them, dates, and project progress. It also integrates with lots of other programs, including Salesforce, Slack, and Google Workspace.

Although Workfront is generally rated well, making tasks and managing projects can sometimes be cumbersome. And although the software allows you to hold discussions and share documents within tasks, it's not always easy to find the content you're looking for. With that in mind, it may not be ideal for companies that use their project management tool for most of their collaboration and sharing.

Wrike

Full disclosure, Wrike is one of my personal favorites. It's the one I usually choose when companies retain me as their digital marketing consultant. It's quite intuitive once it's set up, and teams tend to adapt to it rapidly. Plus, you have a high degree of control over who sees what, which is beneficial if you're blending an in-house team with outsourced talent.

As a collaboration tool, Wrike has options like communication within tasks, document sharing, approval processes, and a native editor for tracking change requests and versions. The platform also has more than 400 integrations with software like Salesforce. Marketo, and Google Workspace, so it's easier to keep everything integrated and together.

If there's a major fault with the platform, it's that it can be difficult to get set up. Creating your workflows and templates in a way that makes sense, streamlines your work, and provides for easy tracking isn't always straightforward if you haven't done it before.

Getting Started

Your project management tool will literally become part of everything your marketing team does, including both in-house and outsourced roles, so it influences everything from morale to results. If you already have people on board, include them in the discussion. Many of the tools mentioned here also offer free trials or free versions, so you can set up an account and create dummy projects for everyone involved to explore. While you want to start using your chosen tool as soon as possible to start reaping all the benefits, take time to thoroughly evaluate it before full adoption and make sure the tool you choose works for your needs.

[i] CoSchedule. "Trend Report: Marketing Strategy." CoSchedule. https://bit.ly/dmo-8-i

Chapter 9

Password Management

You've probably noticed that this book is filled with tools and programs that successful marketing teams leverage. It becomes even more nuanced as we move into individual roles you may fill through outsourcing. That means there will be a lot of passwords in use and the number will grow even more as you scale. If your marketing team isn't using an enterprise password management tool yet, it should be. Not only can one save you an immense amount of time, but it may be the very thing that prevents your company from going out of business.

How Password Managers Work

Password managers are encrypted digital vaults that store your login credentials to save you the trouble of remembering multiple complex passwords and give you peace of mind. While capabilities differ across platforms, many will automatically fill forms for you, suggest strong passwords, and help keep your sensitive data protected from cybercriminals too.

The concept can be further split into privileged user password management, which is more of an enterprise-level technology type. Instead of simply helping manage passwords, privileged user systems monitor all programs. Some can tell you which passwords your employees are using in programs outside of your password manager, help ensure regulatory compliance, and more.

Dangers of Leaving Password Management to Team Members

Each login to your marketing tools presents some risk, so the larger your team grows, the opportunities for hackers to gain access increase too. Keep the following in mind if you're on the fence about whether your team really needs a password manager.

People are bad at creating passwords.

Consider that 23 million account holders use the password "123456" and the average password has eight or fewer characters[i]. That means a brute force hacker can be in the account within eight hours, while most passwords take an hour or less to crack[ii].

People recycle passwords.

Despite being the least likely group to recycle passwords, 60 percent of Baby Boomers do it anyway[iii]. Gen Z takes the lead, with 78 percent sharing passwords across multiple accounts. Considering more than 22 billion records are shared on the dark web each year[iv], at least 13 billion compromised credentials unlock other accounts. In other words, there's a good chance a hacker can get into at least some of a person's other accounts, even if only one set of credentials is leaked.

People use the same passwords for personal use and work.

About half the population recycles passwords between their work and personal accounts, increasing the risk of leaks and breaches. Even if your company forces password updates at pre-determined intervals, most people only change one digit[v]. That's not enough to keep your data and programs safe.

People make mistakes.

Two-thirds of data breaches are "inside jobs[vi]." The people behind this latest cybersecurity crisis aren't necessarily bad employees or even trying to let secure info out, but they may unintentionally share things or fall victim to phishing schemes. A password management tool can be a helpful component of a comprehensive access management strategy that eliminates many of these concerns. Plus, some come with helpful tools that can identify many phishing pages designed to steal password information, helping reduce cybersecurity risk even more.

People can be careless.

Without a place to store passwords securely, most people will resort to unsecured methods, such as post-it notes and spreadsheets.

Why Enterprise Password Management is Essential

Password-related challenges grow as your team does. Particularly if you're outsourcing and people are using their own internet connections, equipment, and so forth, a good password management tool addresses even more concerns.

Marketing teams use lots of tools and therefore have lots of passwords.

The average marketer uses 12 different tools, while nearly one in ten uses 31 or more tools[vii]. This can be overwhelming by itself, but bear in mind the figures only reference marketing tools such as social media accounts, email marketing platforms, and CRMs. It doesn't include project management tools, time tracking apps, file management programs, and so forth that add to the total number of passwords a marketing team needs. Let's face it. If you're not using a password management tool and you have this many accounts, there's no way you're using unique and difficult-to-crack passwords across them all and refreshing them as needed to keep hackers out. Single sign-on (SSO) options help, but not all platforms offer them, and SSO doesn't help with all the human-caused issues.

Hacking is a major concern.

Almost 50 percent of small businesses have been cyber-attack victims[viii]. Within six months of an attack, up to 60 percent will go out of business. Passwords are an easy target in this regard. Simply put, your company needs more security than your employees or a traditional tool can provide.

Password management tools keep your company in control.

Enterprise password management tools give your company more control over the types of passwords being used and who has access to what. Some will even allow you to share a password or groups of passwords with a user but not give them the actual password. This is helpful if your whole team uses a single login for a program that doesn't require the security afforded by separate logins, such as certain design programs. It's easy to remove access as needed to safeguard your data when individuals leave the company too.

Your marketing efforts and company reputation could be lost in a single breach.

Imagine waking up one morning to find your social media accounts littered with posts you didn't make, your outboxes filled with messages to your clients that you didn't send, or your website loaded down with malicious pages. It doesn't matter if the hacker never got sensitive data. Trust will erode, you may lose business, and your ranking on search engines like Google may tank, or your listing may come with a warning that the site's been hacked. As the outward face of your company, your marketing team must be especially cautious to avoid a breach.

Features to Look for in a Password Management Solution

Reputable platforms will base their password requirements around the National Institute of Standards and Technology (NIST) guidelines. As it's the primary standards organization of the United States and sets the information security standards for federal agencies, it's the one to look to if your organization must be compliant with guidelines like HIPAA, FISMA, and SOX. In addition, the agency issued digital authentication guidelines that include details such as having an eight-character minimum for user-generated passwords and allowing users up to at least 64 characters.

Beyond NIST adherence, you'll want to look for features that enhance security and make password management easier. A few examples are covered below.

Your platform should work across multiple operating systems.

At a bare minimum, the password manager should work on Windows, Mac, Android, and Apple devices. Considering outsourced talent will provide their own devices, and many in-house team members will use personal devices too, there's no telling what anyone might be using at any given time.

A cloud-based vault should be leveraged.

Although the most popular options are all cloud-based, it's worth double-checking that the one you're choosing is, so you don't have to worry about syncing or which devices have which passwords.

Password generator tools are a must.

Remember that most manually created passwords can be cracked in under an hour. A good password generator will suggest secure passwords that will take years to crack.

Admin control over password recovery for the tool is necessary.

Each user will have his or her own master password that provides access to the tool. For ease of use, you may want a self-service password recovery option that allows employees to reset their own forgotten passwords, but it's also helpful to have a password reset option at the admin level too.

Think beyond single-layer security.

Consider choosing a service that uses two-factor authentication or multi-factor authentication for enhanced security.

Password encryption adds more security.

End-to-end or zero trust encryption is another big one, as it keeps passwords encrypted while they're not being used and while they're being sent, so your data is even safer.

Consider data storage if your team shares sensitive docs.

If your team routinely shares privileged items like contracts, you may want to select an option with file storage and sharing.

Password sharing may be beneficial for some teams.

Certain tools your team leverages, such as social media logins and CRM logins, really should be tied to each user. That way, you can easily see who touched what if an audit is needed. However, if you work with programs that aren't sensitive, the ability to share passwords or groups of passwords based on someone's role can be a huge timesaver.

Commonly Used Password Management Solutions

Now that we've covered what password management solutions do and how they can help your marketing team, let's look at some of the actual tools you'll find.

1Password Business

One of the best-known platforms is 1Password. It offers integration with other business tools and has a multitude of features. There are options to purchase by the user or in groups, as well as a free trial.

BeyondTrust

Often listed alongside business password management tools, BeyondTrust is actually privileged access management software (PAM). While it does offer password management, it also gives more robust tools intended for use by an IT department, such as analytics, session logging, and enhanced monitoring. For example, in monitoring privileged accounts, it helps keep your company protected against more data breaches.

Bitwarden

One that gets a fair amount of press for being free is Bitwarden. As one would imagine, the free version is fairly stripped down and cuts off at two users. However, it has a good reputation and isn't a bad place to start if your team is very small or doesn't require advanced features.

Centrify Enterprise

Like Beyond Trust, Centrify falls within the privileged access management software bracket. While it will manage your passwords, it hangs its hat on safeguarding your company against privileged access abuse. That means the software is always monitoring users who have been granted access to things to ensure they're using them within the scope of their intended purpose or role and that they're not performing actions that could put the company at risk.

CommonKey | Team Password Manager

One of the latest products to hit the market is CommonKey. It works differently than many of the others outlined here because it's purely a browser extension designed to work with your cloud-based applications. It offers most of the features some of the larger platforms do, such as easy management of your team, and it has a user-friendly interface. Although it's not compatible with all major browsers yet, it's one of the most affordable options, and there's an option to get started free.

Dashlane

Most teams want a cloud-based vault with automatic syncing between devices to save time and headaches. However, if you're the type that feels better keeping your passwords locally, Dashlane is worth a look. The admin dashboard also has a panel that shows you the password health of your team members and details like who is using weak passwords. It also has an active directory of compromised passwords and alerts you if a team member is using one.

Keeper Security

If you're looking at the more robust platforms, Keeper Security might be worth a look too. It sets itself apart with easy deployment of passwords across groups and works with some unique operating systems, including Kindle and Blackberry, in addition to the more common ones.

LastPass Enterprise

Over the years, 1Password and LastPass have been fighting neck-and-neck. When one tops the other in an area, the trailing one does an update that matches it or beats it. The two are comparably priced and offer many of the same features, and both have free trials. However, LastPass offers a password import option, and its Windows interface is sometimes considered superior.

ManageEngine

You may hear the name ManageEngine while you're searching too. It's another privileged access management software provider that runs neck-and-neck with Centrify. However, users typically rate it a little lower on features and a little better for pricing.

Pleasant Password Server

If you're a DIYer with technical prowess or have an IT department, you can use Pleasant Password Server with KeePass or Password Safe to create a more customized and locally hosted solution.

RoboForm For Business

If you're looking at options like 1Password and LastPass but don't like the price, you might be happy with RoboForm. It offers all the basic password management tools for teams for just a few dollars per month.

Zoho Vault Online Password Manager for Teams

Zoho offers a huge suite of tools that can either be purchased individually or as a group under the Zoho One name. The latter includes everything from website builders through to Customer Relationship Management (CRM) and email marketing tools. So, if you're a Zoho One user, you can use Zoho Vault without paying anything extra, or you can purchase it individually fairly inexpensively. The company tries to contend with companies like LastPass and 1Password, but their program doesn't quite have the same ease of use. It does, however, integrate with other password tools. That means if you need mobile device password protection and your current service doesn't offer it, but you don't want to switch, Zoho Vault may give you the functionality you need.

Getting Started

Even though there are many password management tools to choose from, this isn't the same kind of undertaking as selecting a project management tool. Most password managers run quietly in the background and aren't something your team will think about much, if at all.

However, you want this layer of security in place before you start bringing in freelancers because it will be far easier to implement when it's done at an early stage, and the team will benefit from features like password generators as they're setting up their initial accounts.

 [i] Ivana Vojinovic. "Save Your Data with These Empowering Password Statistics." DataProt. https://bit.ly/dmo-9-i

 [ii] Charlie Fripp. "Use this chart to see how long it'll take to crack your passwords." Kim Komando. https://bit.ly/dmo-9-ii

 [iii] Johnny Lieu. "Young people are overconfident with online security, survey suggests." The Harris Poll. https://bit.ly/dmo-9-iii

 [iv] ITP Staff. "Over 22 billion records were exposed in data breaches: report." ITP net. https://bit.ly/dmo-9-iv

 [v] Lani Leuthvilay. "Password Usage Study: A Conversation with Yan Grinshtein." Hypr. https://bit.ly/dmo-9-v

[vi] Amanda Glassner. "Negligent Employees, Accidental Data Breaches Rising."Cybersecurity Magazine. https://bit.ly/dmo-9-vi

 [vii] Jami Oetting. "Too Many Tools? New Data on the Complexity of Marketing Technology." HubSpot. https://bit.ly/dmo-9-vii

 [viii] Thomas Koulopoulos. "60 Percent of Companies Fail in 6 Months Because of This (It's Not What You Think)." Inc. Magazine. https://bit.ly/dmo-9-viii

Chapter 10

How to NOT Waste Money on Content Marketing

As we explored in the digital marketing tree, content marketing will be one of your earliest digital marketing initiatives, second only to your website and email marketing. You may have also noticed that when we covered content marketing calendars, I gave some general guidelines for content production across various channels but also acknowledged that volume varies by goal and that quality should be your focus. There's a reason for this.

There's a common misconception that content marketing is all about producing blogs at breakneck speeds. You'll hear varying "helpful" tips about content marketing that you should blog three times a week or even daily to achieve results. This is not ideal as it can increase the cost of content marketing and diverts resources from other vital projects.

That's resources wasted regardless of your talent source, but it can be particularly painful when you're outsourcing because you're more conscious of what each piece of content costs to produce. You're not simply paying a salary or sending out a check for hours worked as you do with in-house talent. You know exactly what you're paying your graphic designer, writer, or other professional for each project. Don't think of that as a negative toward outsourcing— it's a benefit because you're more mindful of your marketing spend and therefore use your resources more wisely!

Rather than focus on an arbitrary content count, what you want to do is maximize the value you're getting from each piece of content created. True, the volume should increase as your marketing initiatives scale, but if you're focused on quality and maximizing value, content marketing can help you connect with your audience and boost revenue in a cost-effective way. This chapter will explain how to do just that.

Know Your Audience

People connect with content in different ways. For example, an older audience of business professionals will likely be interested in deep-dive reports that relate to their industry. Younger audiences are trending toward videos and other visual depictions of information.

Before you start developing content, create buyer personas to help you develop content your audience will consume. Include:

- Demographic Information
- Behavior
- Motivation
- Goals
- Pain Points
- Buying Patterns

Know Your Channels

Use buyer personas to identify the best channels to share your content. For example, LinkedIn might be the best place to reach business professionals, while Millennials and Gen Z prefer networks like Twitter and TikTok. Spend more time on the channels your audience frequent.

When you've selected the relevant networks, review the type of content shared on each and the standards each community sets. For example, a single line with a link and image may be ideal for your Twitter audience, but your Facebook audience is going to engage more when your posts are more descriptive. On Instagram, it's all about the visual aspect of the post, so you'll want something unique and eye-catching.

Keep the Momentum Going

Businesses often quit on social media because they do not get the results they expected. It's not that social media doesn't work. It takes time to build your audience. Plus, you're dealing with algorithms that only show your content to a portion of your audience as well as incredibly short lifespans on posts due to the deluge of content that is published on social media. To address these challenges, try the following:

- Make use of automation software that allows you to queue up posts in advance to save time and gain access to content analytics.
- Create a posting schedule/calendar to ensure your audience always has fresh things to view.
- Introduce the same high-quality content in various ways to increase reach and get more exposure from blogs.
- Watch for patterns in what people respond to and repeat your successes.
- Use tags to help more people and search engines to find your posts.
- Follow relevant organizations and influencers.
- Reshare and comment on other content to increase brand awareness.

Give it a Boost

Virtually all social networking platforms allow organizations to pay to have their social posts seen by a wider internet audience. For example, Facebook has a Boost option, LinkedIn does

Sponsored Content, and Twitter has Promoted Tweets. These tools can prove invaluable when you're just starting out and want to cultivate a following, as well as when you're trying to expand your reach as you go.

Engage with Your Audience

Social networks enable brands to start conversations with their followers. If a visitor responds to your post, reply back. Let them know you're interested in what they have to say and make it a two-way dialogue. To expand your network, do some outreach, and find relevant posts from others to comment on and share.

Reuse, Recycle & Repurpose

Think of your content creation like gold; a precious metal that can be endlessly recycled without ever losing quality or degrading. Today, it might be a bar. Tomorrow, it could be a coin or ring. You can use the same content over and over again, giving you more ROI and saving time. Come up with your own ideas or consider some of the following:

- Start with a long piece of quality content or a list and break down the various components into smaller pieces.
- Consolidate blogs, white papers, and case studies on a selected topic and convert them into an e-book.
- Convert the information in your blog posts into other forms of media, such as infographics, webinars, or videos.
- Repost your content on sites like Medium, Mashable, or niche-specific sites that cater to your audience to expand your reach.
- Go through old posts and pick some of the highlights to share on social media. As long as it's still relevant today, it'll continue generating interest.

Getting Started

Content audits will be handled by your digital marketing manager in most cases. As companies grow, they sometimes recruit content marketing managers or have similar roles take responsibility for their content marketing. However, you shouldn't assume the individual is following best practices. Touch base with them to explore their approach and make sure they have access to content created before they are offered the position to ensure it's getting the attention it deserves too.

Chapter 11

Should You Outsource Copywriting or Keep it In-House?

At this point, you should understand the foundations of digital marketing, including channels, budgeting, and some basic tools you'll need. You should also have your digital marketing manager on board or at least identified how you plan to source and work with one. It's now time to start creating your digital marketing team of experts.

Again, not every role should be outsourced. High-performing digital marketing teams typically use a blend of in-house and outsourced talent. That blend will look somewhat different within each organization. My goal in this and subsequent chapters is not to convince you to outsource, but rather, to help you apply the strategies I use as a digital marketing consultant to ensure each role is filled in a way that best supports the business's needs and goals.

We've focused quite a bit on content thus far, so it's probably no surprise the first role we discuss after management is that of your copywriter.

The Role of a Copywriter

You will see a distinction between "copywriter" and "content writer" when you're filling this role. Copywriters write persuasively with the intent to sell your product or service. A copywriter crafts things like ads, landing pages, and brochures. Content writers focus more on informational materials. A content writer creates things like blogs and newsletters.

Most small and midsized businesses only need one writer to start with. Limiting yourself to one writer at the beginning shortens the learning curve and ensures your marketing materials have greater consistency too. With that in mind, I blend the two roles in this chapter, just as you'll do when you're filling your first writing role. You can fill the role with someone who refers to themselves by either term, so long as they can perform the necessary tasks.

Core Competencies and Resources

Many people on your team can probably write, but that doesn't necessarily make them writers, nor does it mean they enjoy writing, have the ability to create quality copy, or have the bandwidth to do so. It's important to have a professional writer on your team who is dedicated to the role for these reasons.

A good copywriter will have a diverse skill set.

Skills to look for include:

- Ability to write high-quality, reader-friendly, concise, compelling, grammatically correct copy

- Ability to maintain brand standards and be consistent
- An understanding of the market and audience
- Ability to tailor copy to readers in terms of language, style, and medium
- An understanding of SEO (search engine optimization) and web markups

Copywriters should know how to work with various tools.

Although your copywriter may be able to get by with only a word processing program, chances are they will need access to a variety of tools to enhance quality and aid in collaboration.

- Proofreading and editing tools (Grammarly, WhiteSmoke, etc.)
- Analytics (Google, your CRM, etc.)
- Collaboration and project management (Google Docs, Wrike, Asana, etc.)
- Images (Canva, Pexels, Flickr, Shutterstock, etc.)

Your copywriter must have enough time to devote to the job.

One of the challenges of keeping your copywriting in-house is that companies have the tendency to assign someone the task of creating copy, but it's not necessarily what they do, and it's low on their priority list of duties.

It takes time to create quality copy, so make sure whoever's handling your copywriting has enough of this resource to do the work well. Equally, you may not need a full-time copywriter. If so, that's ok too. You can always hire a professional copywriter for a part-time position. The key here is to ensure that whoever is on the task has the bandwidth to dedicate to it.

Identifying Success in Copywriting

In short, a copywriter is successful if the end-user or visitor takes whatever action you hope they'll take. KPIs look different depending on what type of project the copywriter is working on, but there is always some way to measure the success.

Use KPIs to measure success.

- ROI
- Cost per acquisition
- Conversion rates
- Open rates and click-through rates
- Time on page

Making the Final Decision

Ultimately, if your company has the resources necessary to keep copywriting in-house, you're measuring the success of the copy, and you are happy with the results, there's no reason to outsource the role. However, if you're struggling to find someone with the skills you need or aren't getting results from your copy, it's a good idea to explore outsourcing it.

Chapter 12

Should You Outsource Social Media Marketing or Keep it In-House?

No matter where you do business or who your customers are, chances are they're online. Nearly three-quarters of Americans are on various social media platforms[i], and approximately three billion people worldwide are tapped into the trend[ii].

Connecting with your target audience and boosting brand awareness in the places they already frequent is a natural fit for marketing. Plus, social media marketing is one of the easiest strategies to implement, has one of the lowest minimum investments, and it scales with you. That's why it's in the "low-hanging fruit" category on the digital marketing tree and why you'll be filling your social media marketing role as one of your first initiatives too.

The Role of a Social Media Marketer

Often referred to as a social media manager, not because of seniority, but because they actively manage your social media accounts, your social media marketing professional wears many hats. On the one hand, they're building brand awareness by creating a calendar full of compelling posts to encourage potential customers to follow your brand and interact. On the other, they're connecting with influencers, keeping an eye on your competitors' posts, building relationships by talking to your customers, performing customer service duties, cultivating engagement, and creating strategic campaigns around your business goals. It's equal parts creative and technical work.

Things happen on social media at breakneck speeds. Tweets, for example, have a half-life of just 18 minutes[iii]. That means a tweet will get half of all the retweets it will ever receive within minutes of posting. Facebook and other social networks such as Pinterest, Instagram, LinkedIn, etc., don't fare much better. Plus, more than 80 percent of people expect a brand to respond to them within 24 hours[iv], a window that is much shorter with certain demographics, and half say they'll drop a company that doesn't respond to a negative post. In other words, there's a lot riding on having frequent interactions as well as swift, appropriate responses on social media.

Core Competencies and Resources

There are many companies that specialize in outsourced social media marketing, and they often promise measurable results. These companies may not like my response, but I believe social media marketing is one component of your digital marketing that generally should not be outsourced because they're unable to deliver in one or more of the key areas covered below.

An effective social media marketer will have a diverse skill set.

Skills to look for include:

- An understanding of your brand
- An understanding of your target audience
- Ability to tailor content to the network and audience
- Familiarity with A/B testing and analytics
- Comfort with AI and automation
- Familiarity with SEO and keywords
- An understanding of each network, Including best practices and demographics
- Comfort creating a variety of content types, from copy to images and video
- Communication
- Video and image design

Social media marketers should know how to work with various tools.

Some of the most common tools leveraged include:

- Scheduling and posting (Buffer, Sprout Social, Hootsuite, etc.)
- Images (Canva, Pexels, Flickr, Shutterstock, etc.)

- Videos (Animoto, Adobe Spark, etc.)
- Trending content and influencer discovery (BuzzSumo, Ahrefs, Mention, etc.)
- Trending topics (Google Trends, Ubersuggest, Ahrefs, WordStream, etc.)
- Proofreading and editing (Grammarly, WhiteSmoke, etc.)
- Analytics (Google, your posting tool, native network tools, etc.)
- Collaboration and project management (Google Docs, Wrike, Asana, etc.)

Your social media marketer must be tuned into your channels at the right times.

The total time necessary to successfully manage your social media marketing will naturally scale with your organization and number of followers. For example, a midsize company may only need someone manning social media for 20-25 hours per week. As things ramp up and your audience comes to rely on your channels, it will become a full-time job within your marketing team. Large corporations have teams to monitor social media efforts around the clock.

Identifying Success in Social Media Marketing

Although building relationships through social media marketing may seem a bit intangible, there are many ways to measure how effective your marketing plan and social media strategy is. You may use some KPIs all the time and others just as you're running campaigns or working toward specific goals.

Use KPIs to measure success.

- Impressions
- Reach
- Comments
- Likes
- Shares
- Mentions
- Sentiment
- Conversion rate
- Click-through rate (CTR)
- Audience Growth
- Cost-per-click (CPC)
- Cost per thousand impressions (CPM)

Making the Final Decision

You will find agencies and freelancers who promise to grow your audience exponentially, and some of them can deliver in this respect. However, it's important to consider how your audience is engaging with your brand on social media. They want current information, fast responses, and personalized service from someone who knows them and the brand inside and out. In order for your social media manager to provide all this, they need to have a pulse on your company and be active at least daily.

Can an outsourced provider deliver in this respect? Probably not. It's virtually impossible for someone to be the immediate voice of your company when they're removed from it. With that in mind, your social media marketing role should almost always be kept in-house.

[i] Pew Research Center. "Social Media Fact Sheet." Pew Research. https://bit.ly/dmo-12-i

 [ii] Statista. "Number of social network users worldwide." Statista. https://bit.ly/dmo-12-ii

 [iii] Peter Bray. "When Is My Tweet's Prime of Life? (A brief statistical interlude.)" Moz. https://bit.ly/dmo-12-iii

 [iv] Swetha Amaresan. "What Are Your Customers' Expectations for Social Media Response Time?" HubSpot. https://bit.ly/dmo-12-iv

Chapter 13

Should You Outsource Your Search Engine Optimization or Keep it In-House?

Google processes more than 40,000 searches every second, which amounts to some 1.2 trillion searches globally each year[i]. While it attracts the largest number of searchers, capturing more than three-quarters of traffic[ii], others, such as Baidu, Yahoo, Yandex, and Bing present significant opportunities for businesses too.

Search engine optimization (SEO) refers to a series of activities related to, or the process of, helping a website appear in more of these searches and getting a site to display at the top of the search results.

The payout for a well-optimized site can be huge—literally delivering millions of visitors to a site each month. However, I categorize SEO as mid-range fruit in the digital marketing tree because the investment is greater than that of low-hanging fruit and it typically takes some time before organic traffic starts rolling in from your efforts.

A professional who performs tasks related to this goal may simply be referred to as an "SEO." Titles such as "SEO Expert," "SEO Specialist," or "SEO Strategist" are also common. Any of these roles, or the individual activities the professionals may engage in to boost search engine rankings, may be kept in-house or outsourced.

SEO Roles

Because SEO is a multifaceted job that is typically handled by a full team, it makes more sense to look at the individual SEO roles a company may require rather than the process as a whole.

Keyword Research

Keywords are the phrases people type into search engines when they're looking for some information. During keyword research, a specialist evaluates the actual words people search for, identifies which ones align with the business and its goals, and determines how challenging any given keyword would be to rank well in search engines.

Although the task doesn't need to be done often, keywords should be evaluated regularly to ensure any new ones are being leveraged and that those being used are still a good fit for the business.

Competitor Research

Speaking in general terms, I tell businesses not to worry too much about what their competitors are doing in their digital marketing or online strategies. It can cause them to lose sight of their own identity and branding. However, when it comes to SEO, it's always a good idea to investigate what competitors are doing. By using this tactic, you know which areas are already saturated by the competition and which opportunities you can capitalize on with greater ease.

Analytics

I cover the digital marketing analyst's role separately in a later chapter because it truly is its own role. However, to know whether your optimization efforts are working, your analyst must be able to report on various aspects of SEO. You'll see more on how these roles are intertwined in a moment in the section on SEO KPIs too.

Strategy

Using research and analytics, an SEO strategist creates a roadmap of activities to improve the website's optimization. As with keyword and competitor research, there's a large time investment at the onset, though as plans are carried out, it becomes more a matter of monitoring the results and making adjustments as needed.

Link Optimization

The links on your pages—whether they work, where they lead, and the words that are linked— impact how search engines view your site. A link optimization expert will explore your current links to ensure they're providing you maximum value and find opportunities to improve on-page links.

Outreach

Another factor in SEO is your website's perceived popularity or reputation. Whereas companies in the past tried to game the system by buying links or having links placed on lots of low-quality/ spammy sites, these techniques no longer work and can even harm your ranking today. Outreach specialists help you get high-quality backlinks on reputable websites through things like article placement/ guest posting, providing quotes for articles, and maintaining local listings.

Development

Like analytics, the role of a developer is covered independently in a later chapter. Many development tasks do not have SEO components, but quite a few do. For example, the structure of your URLs impacts SEO, as does page load times, how pages are coded, .htaccess and robots.txt files, and metadata too. These things may be addressed by your developer or by a technical SEO specialist.

Content Marketing

All your content may not need to be optimized, but things like your blogs, social media, and web pages will get much more exposure if they're written with SEO best practices in mind and leverage a keyword strategy. This is why SEO was listed as a skill in the chapter on copywriting.

Core Competencies and Resources

The skills and resources required for SEO will vary based on the role and task at hand. A well-rounded SEO team will possess a wide range of skills and leverage many tools.

Each SEO role will require a different skill set.

Some examples of common SEO skills include:

- Technical SEO
- On-page SEO
- Local SEO
- Mobile SEO
- Coding (HTML, CSS, JavaScript)

- Keyword research
- Analytics and metrics
- Familiarity with various search engines and ranking factors

SEO professionals work with various tools.

A few common SEO tools include:

- Google Tools (Google Analytics, Google Search Console)
- Moz
- SEMrush
- Ahrefs
- Brightedge
- Majestic

The time investment will vary by SEO activity.

SEO is not something you can tackle quickly; it takes time to produce results. Some SEO tasks aren't done repetitively either. Your research, for example, will be performed once and then left for a while. Your technical SEO aspects may also be short-term work.

Conversely, your link-building and content will likely be continuous, with analytics providing regular insights as to how the work is going. Depending on the scale of your SEO strategy, some of these aspects are full-time jobs by themselves, while other aspects may be project-based or part-time.

Identifying Success in SEO

In a perfect world, your team will draft a well, optimized page that leverages a keyword none of your competitors are using. That page will appear in search results within an hour and will start sending traffic to your site right away. The reality is much different.

It may take Google days or weeks to even look at or index the page. Your team can take steps to make sure Google knows the page is there, but it can't force search engines to crawl or index it. This may take weeks to happen.

If you're facing other challenges, such as competitors using the same keyword, technical issues on your site, or lack of trust signals, search engines won't view your page as the most reliable source of information on the topic. It can take your SEO team months of work before you start to see results.

Particularly in the early days of kicking off an SEO strategy, you want to focus more on measuring things like error resolution and tasks completed versus increased traffic. A few general KPIs for SEO campaigns are provided as examples.

Use KPIs to measure success.

- Number of organic sessions
- Increases in keyword ranking
- Crawl errors
- Bounce rate
- Page bounce rate
- Backlinks
- Broken links
- Domain authority increases

Making the Final Decision

Although you might be able to find a single "SEO Specialist" who can perform all necessary SEO tasks, more often than not, SEO professionals excel in a single area. It takes a team to audit and optimize a site well, and it would be overkill for most companies to hire a full in-house SEO team. With that in mind, you'll likely get better results produced more efficiently and cost-effectively if you outsource to a specialized SEO agency.

[i] Internet Live Stats. "Google Search Statistics." Internet Live Stats. https://bit.ly/dmo-13-i

[ii] Internet Live Stats. "Google Search Statistics." Internet Live Stats. https://bit.ly/dmo-13-ii

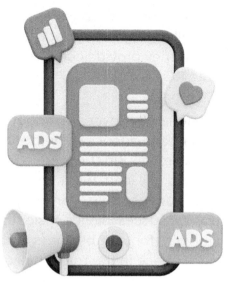

Chapter 14

Should You Outsource Pay-Per-Click or Keep it In-House?

Pay-per-click (PPC) ads are one of the few digital marketing channels that can start working as soon as they're set up and immediately deliver customers who are ready to take action straight to your door.

I'm a big believer in the power of digital ads and PPC advertising for this reason. However, as someone who used to teach Google Partners (marketing firms certified by the search engine to set up ad campaigns for businesses), I also know how challenging it is to get them handled right to ensure they provide consistent results and generate ROI.

This is why I generally advocate for outsourcing PPC to a specialized agency rather than keeping the role in-house, though there are a few caveats. In this chapter, you'll learn what it takes to generate ROI from your PPC campaigns and how to measure success, so it's easier to find the best path forward for your business and ensure whomever you place in the role is delivering the results you expect.

The Role of a PPC Specialist

Many people think of Google and Google Ads when they think of PPC. While the search engine giant certainly dominates the market, it's far from being the only player in the game. Virtually every social media network has its own PPC ad platform, as do other search engines. A multitude of smaller or independent PPC platforms exists too. Your PPC specialist should be knowledgeable in Google Ads (formerly known as Google AdWords) and familiar with some of the alternatives like Bing, Yahoo, and Amazon for this reason.

The platform and type of PPC ad being run largely determine what skills are necessary. In most campaigns, a PPC specialist performs keyword research to see what words and phrases people are interested in that relate to the business and its objectives, then creates ads around them and establishes how much the company is willing to pay to have their ad seen or clicked on.

In addition, PPC specialists monitor for trends or algorithm changes, keep an eye on analytics to see how ads are performing, and engage in A/B testing, so they can adapt the advertising strategy and improve results over time. They're also involved in the creation of ad copy, graphics, and specialized landing pages that encourage those who click to take the next step in your funnel.

Core Competencies and Resources

Effective PPC specialists are highly analytical and have a deep understanding of consumer behavior as well as the platforms they leverage.

An effective PPC specialist will have a diverse skill set.

Skills to look for include:

- Keyword research
- A/B testing
- Analytics
- Copywriting (unless working with a writer)
- Retargeting/ remarketing campaigns
- Landing page design (unless working with a designer/ developer)
- An understanding of the customer journey and funnels
- Ability to work with buyer personas
- An understanding of the business and objectives
- Bid optimization
- Ability to perform a competitor analysis

PPC specialists should know how to work with various tools.

Some of the most common tools leveraged include:

- Platform-specific ad editing tools (Google, Bing, Facebook, LinkedIn, etc.)
- Ad performance enhancement (AdEspresso, WordStream, etc.)
- Competitor research (SEMrush, Spyfu)

- Landing page design (HubSpot, Unbounce, etc.)
- Graphic creation (Canva, gifntext, etc.)
- Setup and maintenance times will vary.

The amount of time spent on PPC will vary depending on your total ad spend and how the ads are performing. Some companies could spend ten or more hours per week on PPC management, while others might only spend ten in a month.

Identifying Success in PPC

There are many ways to measure the effectiveness of PPC campaigns and the person you have managing them.

Use KPIs to measure success.

- Total clicks
- Click-through rate (CTR)
- Cost per click (CPC)
- Conversion rate (CVR)
- Cost per conversion/acquisition (CPA)
- Cost per mille (CPM)
- Impression share

- Ad quality score
- Making the Final Decision

Multiple skill sets are required to manage pay-per-click campaigns effectively, and a specialist must keep their skills sharp to produce results. That's challenging to do if you're just spending a few hours per week on the task, let alone if you're only devoting a couple of hours per month. That's what typically happens when PPC ads are managed in-house, which makes it difficult to get ROI.

With this in mind, it's probably best to outsource PPC campaign management to a specialized PPC management agency. You're more likely to find a team with deep expertise that has homed in their skills, knows what converts, follows the trends, and can get you cost-effective results.

Chapter 15

Should You Outsource Email Marketing or Keep it In-House?

When done right, email marketing delivers as much as $44 for each $1 spent[i], but the average is much less. That's because not every business sending emails has it down to a science, and others are downright sending spam. Your profitability and business growth hinge on making the right personnel choice.

But what is the right choice? Unlike other aspects of digital marketing that should really be handled by an in-house team that knows the brand and lives its mission, or others that may yield better ROI and results if outsourced, how you engage in email marketing is more about finding the right fit for your company.

The Role of an Email Marketer

Email marketers nurture and convert leads through email campaigns. Their work involves creating email lists and segments for targeted campaigns as well as keeping lists clean to maintain high delivery rates. On any given day, an email marketer may be creating email blasts that go out to a large group at once, working on drip campaigns that build relationships over a period of time or crafting newsletters to boost engagement. They monitor the results of campaigns and adjust messaging to improve results on subsequent sends too.

Core Competencies and Resources

Although it may seem like an email marketer's job is primarily focused on content marketing and creating compelling emails, it's a very tech-heavy role these days. In order to get the right message to the right person at the right time, your email marketing professional will need to have a data-oriented mindset, have a wide skill set, and be constantly testing new ideas to find ways to improve the results.

An effective email marketer has a diverse skill set.

A few skills effective email marketers possess include:

- An understanding of your brand
- An understanding of your subscribers
- Ability to segment lists and tailor content
- Ability to manage lists effectively
- Expertise in email template design, layout and build
- Familiarity with A/B testing and analytics
- Familiarity with regulatory guidelines and best practices
- Comfortable with AI and automation

- Familiarity with optimization for email clients and mobile
- Knowledge of the sales funnel
- Copywriting (unless your copywriter handles the copy)
- Familiarity with coding and rendering (even if you're using a drag-and-drop email builder)

Email Marketers should know how to work with various tools.

Some of the most common tools leveraged include:

- Email service provider or ESP (ActiveCampaign, Campaign Monitor, Mailchimp, Constant Contact, Pardot, HubSpot, etc.)
- Render testing (Litmus, Email on Acid, EmailReach, etc.)
- Proofreading and Editing (Grammarly, WhiteSmoke, etc.)
- Analytics (Google, your CRM, etc.)
- Collaboration (Google Docs, Wrike, Asana, etc.)
- Images (Canva, Pexels, Flickr, Shutterstock, etc.)

- An email marketer invests 12 hours per campaign.

Email marketing efforts and campaign management can be time-intensive. Most email marketers spend two hours each on strategy and planning, mobile optimization, transmission, reporting, and data, with another two to eight hours on graphic design and content in any given email campaign[ii]. That means just to be "average," you should be spending 12 hours on each campaign. Some of the outliers, perhaps those still coding their emails from scratch and those crafting mega campaigns, are spending more than eight hours on each component. Again, this is for each campaign being run, and chances are your company will schedule several each month on your chosen platform, so it's essential to ensure your email marketing specialist has ample time to carry out all the necessary tasks.

Identifying Success in Email Marketing

Each email marketing campaign is different. In one campaign, maybe your goal will simply be to reengage contacts, while other times, you may want them to update their information or make a purchase. As the email marketing strategy is being refined, you may also place more focus on metrics like how your lists are working, who is actually receiving the emails, and other technical aspects.

Use KPIs to measure success.

- Deliverability rate
- Inbox placement rate (IPR)
- Open rate
- Click-through rate
- Click-to-open rate
- Unsubscribe rate
- Hard and soft bounce rates
- Spam reports
- Social shares
- Forward rate
- Conversion rate
- ROI

Making the Final Decision

As you can see, there are many ways to measure the success of your campaigns and even more things that contribute to their success. If you have someone on your team who understands all these components, or you can find someone and they have the bandwidth to dedicate to email marketing, you can keep your email marketing in-house. However, if you're struggling to find someone with this expertise or you're not getting strong, measurable results, it may be time to look at outsourcing.

---

 [i] Will Harris. "How Do You Calculate Email Marketing ROI?" Campaign Monitor. https://bit.ly/dmo-15-i

 [ii] Henry Hyder-Smith. "Email Marketing Industry Census." Adestra. https://bit.ly/dmo-15-ii

Chapter 16

Should You Outsource Graphic Design and Creative Work or Keep it In-House?

Did you know that people immediately focus their attention on images when they land on a page or open an email? Not only are graphics one of the first things people notice but eye-tracking studies show that visitors spend more time looking at images than they do other elements on the page[i].

This means that the graphics you choose and how they're displayed have a major impact on your overall digital marketing results. Investing in a skilled graphic designer is therefore imperative, but how you source your talent is a matter of what works best for your business.

The Role of Graphic Designer

Designers deliver ROI by helping your business:

- Create a positive first impression
- Build brand recognition
- Communicate effectively
- Create a professional image
- Boost conversions
- Increase trust and goodwill with your audience

Graphic Design Specialties

Graphic designers learn core skills such as color theory, how to communicate via art, and effective layout creation while in school. After that, most focus on one of seven specialty areas.

Product Design

Examples include things like product packaging, marketing designs, and product illustrations.

Branding Design

This includes logos, company letterhead, company brochures, and website branding fit within this bracket.

Website and App Design

People often think of website development and website design as the same thing, but design is more about the user experience (UX) and whether the layout makes sense to a user and guides the person to the intended destination.

Print Design

Brochures, flyers, branded merch (mugs, shirts, etc.).

Publishing Design

eBook layouts, graphs, and book or magazine covers fall in this category.

Environmental Design

Signage, store layouts, and museum exhibits fit into this design type.

Animation Design

A few examples include animated social media graphics, animated explainers, and motion graphics for online videos. If you want your logo to appear animated, such as the way the original Disney logo would appear at the touch of Tinkerbell's wand, this requires the help of an animation designer too.

Core Competencies and Resources

Notice anything missing on the list of specialties? There's no singular niche dedicated to advertising and marketing. It's an area that creatives choose to pursue on their own. Because of this, you'll need to be very specific when you're choosing a graphic designer to ensure the person you select has a firm grasp of marketing-specific graphic design.

The skills needed will vary based on the task at hand.

If you're hiring someone for graphic design and creative work in the field of digital marketing, you'll need to dig deep to find out if their skills are a match for your needs and examine their portfolio carefully. For example, even if someone makes gorgeous sharable social media graphics, they may not be the best choice if you require infographics or a whitepaper. With that in mind, there's no definitive list of skills your creative should have, but the following serves as a baseline:

- Composition
- Branding
- Layout
- Storyboarding
- Typography
- Color theory
- Coding (CSS, HTML, etc.)
- Time management

- Communication
- Problem-solving
- Teamwork
- Analytical mindset
- Willingness to accept constructive feedback

Graphic designers work with lots of different tools.

Tools will vary based on the project and task at hand as well. A few common tools designers use in digital marketing include:

- Photo editing, image creation, and graphic design software (Adobe Photoshop, Pixlr X, etc.)
- Vector graphic design software (Adobe Illustrator, GIMP, etc.)
- Motion graphics and visual effects software (Adobe After Effects, Blender, Nuke, Fusion Studio, etc.)
- Vector animation tools (Adobe Animate, Toonz, Toon Boom, etc.)
- PDF creation tools (Adobe Acrobat, Nitro Pro, Fixit PhantomPDF, etc.)
- Slideshow creation software (PowerPoint, Google Slides, Prezi, Keynote, etc.)

- Proofing and project management tools (ProofHub, Wrike, Asana, etc.)

Identifying Success in Graphic Design

Whether you're outsourcing graphic design and creative work or managing it in-house, being able to measure the success of the work is essential. While certain aspects, such as creativity, are intangible, you can measure design based on areas related to quality, impact, time, and money. Your graphic design KPIs will be unique to your situation and may vary depending on the project or campaign. A few examples are highlighted below.

Graphic design success can be gauged with quality-related KPIs.

- Brand colors, fonts, and other style guide requirements met
- Graphics delivered in required resolution and format
- Files use standardized naming convention
- Graphics and source files archived for later use

- Projects delivered in preferred manner
- Number of revisions

Impact-related KPIs are also an option.

- Conversion rates/ image clicks
- Time on page
- Social media engagement (likes, shares)

Time-related KPIs may be beneficial too.

- Response times
- Delivery times
- Milestones met on time
- Hours spent on revisions

Money-related KPIs are another alternative.

- Project completed within budget
- ROI requirements met

Making the Final Decision

You can keep this role in-house or outsource it. When I'm evaluating the role on behalf of a company I'm consulting to, I look at three key considerations: skills, tools, and time.

Can or does someone on your team have the skills to fulfill the role?

It's good to have a close relationship with your graphic designer. The longer someone works on your materials, the better they'll understand your brand image and branding elements. They'll work quickly, and your materials will also have a more consistent look.

However, professional graphic designers who focus on digital marketing are a small subset, and even if you have one on staff or can find one, they may not have all the skills you need. Because of this, most companies tend to outsource and develop long-term relationships with one or more designers.

Can you provide all the required tools?

You may have noticed Adobe appeared on the list of tools repeatedly. That's not a fluke. Most of the tools mentioned come bundled in the Adobe Creative Suite, which costs more than $7,500 annually for businesses. It's by far the most widely-used solution, and professional designers prefer it. Your creative may need other tools besides this, which will be your responsibility to supply if you opt for in-house talent. Outsourced graphic designers procure their own tools, which is another reason many companies choose to bring on external help.

Does it make sense timewise to have a dedicated design professional?

If your business is at the point where you're considering bringing on a graphic designer, the person generally should be a specialist, not a Jack of all trades. This will ensure you get professional results. It also keeps time wasted to a minimum, as someone who works on graphic design projects all day is going to create pieces much quicker than someone who just does it a couple of times per week or month.

Equally, most businesses don't need a full-time graphic designer. You might have a few hours per week to give someone, but not likely enough to amount to part-time hours, let alone a full-time position. For these reasons, outsourcing graphic design usually works best.

Consider your answers to the above questions carefully.

Generally speaking, it's overkill for most companies, especially small businesses, to have an in-house graphic designer. Particularly if you can develop a long-term relationship with outsourced talent, and this person not only gets to know your brand well but also puts systems in place to ensure consistency as other designers are brought in to fill skills gaps and create other types of content. It's the best of all worlds.

[i] Mike Volpe. "3 Hot Marketing Tips from Heat Map Analysis (images)." HubSpot. https://bit.ly/dmo-16-i

Chapter 17

Should You Outsource Your Apps and Other Development Tasks or Keep Them In-House?

One area people don't always consider with their digital marketing is development projects, such as the company's app or website. They think of development as its own category or an aside from what they're already doing. The reality is that your apps, websites, and similar projects are part of your digital marketing efforts. When they're done well, they're strong tools that can help you attract an audience, build relationships, and create sales. They're digital marketing powerhouses.

However, you will need to have enough resources, office space, and a strong infrastructure to be able to support the development on your own. A lack of expertise in the in-house team can lead to extra costs and time delays too. Outsourcing is generally best for this reason, but we'll take a look at the role in this chapter so it's easier to make the right choice for your business.

The Role of a Developer

Developers, also known as software engineers or coders, are IT professionals who create and maintain websites and applications. They're also responsible for other technical aspects of a build, such as testing and debugging, as well as addressing concerns like performance and capacity. The role varies depending on the task at hand and usually falls into one of four development subsets.

Mobile Application Development

Mobile app development involves creating the codes that make up apps used on mobile devices, including phones and tablets. Some mobile app developers specialize in specific operating systems, such as iOS and Android.

Front-End Development

Front-end developers, also called client-side developers, are focused on the user interface (UI design) and user experience (UX) aspects of a build. They're experts in creating fluid web layouts that people can use intuitively and help both the user and the company achieve their respective goals. They also spend a fair amount of time ensuring that people have a good experience across multiple browsers, operating systems, and devices.

Back-End Development

Also referred to as a server-side developer, a back-end developer is concerned with the internal workings of a project. To give some context, when you use something like Google, the portions you're clicking on, and the box you're typing in are designed by a front-end developer. It's the back-end development team that created the engine itself—the portions that know what to look for and decide which results you're going to see.

Full-Stack Development

Full-stack developers cover both front-end and back-end development tasks. They can create an entire website or app from scratch alone.

Core Competencies and Resources

Because development is an umbrella term with a wide array of skills and resources required within each subset, you'll need to consider the task at hand and ask to see samples of similar work when you're hiring. Just as we saw with graphic design, skills in one area may not readily translate to skills in another. For example, you may find a fantastic front-end developer who makes beautiful, intuitive websites that convert leads. However, if your company later needs something specialized, such as an e-commerce portal or option for customers to log in and pay their bills, you might need to bring in a back-end or full-stack developer too. Because of this, there's no definitive list of skills your developer should have, but the following serves as a baseline.

Developers should possess common core skills.

Skills to look for include:

- Proficiency in multiple programming languages
- Comfort with data structures and algorithms
- Source control
- Data analysis
- Database knowledge
- At least a basic understanding of networking
- Comfortable with AI and automation
- Testing
- Problem Solving
- Communication
- An understanding of your brand, customers, and objectives

Experienced developers should know how to work with various tools.

Some of the most common tools leveraged include:

- Integrated developer environments (IDEs)
- Code review and management
- Code debugging and editing
- Testing
- Analytics
- Collaboration and project management

Time investments will vary based on the project.

The amount of time a developer needs to complete a project will vary greatly from one task to the next. For example, a good developer can customize a pre-built website or application in less than a day, provided you're only looking for basic edits.

Companies with greater customization needs, such as a startup, and those that need something built completely from scratch to suit their needs will naturally require much more time. However, the investment could be anything from days to years, depending on the specifications.

Having an outsourced team of professionals who know how to leverage project management platforms and tools such as agile methodology to stay within your schedules and timelines while increasing flexibility and aiming for continuous improvements. This can produce the high-quality software products your company desires.

Identifying Success in Development

Successful development usually means meeting or exceeding expectations in three core areas; quality, effectiveness, and productivity. However, the KPIs your organization uses to measure success will vary based on your goals and long-term strategy. A few examples are highlighted below.

Use KPIs to measure success.

- Milestones met on time
- Percent to completion of a project
- Lines of code delivered
- Number of dual-purpose solutions created

- Number of bugs reported and/or eliminated
- Number of issues and/or critical issues solved
- Comprehensiveness of documentation

Making the Final Decision

As you can see, application development is complex, both in terms of the physical creation, as well as in the management of the projects. However, most companies don't have a lot of ongoing development work. Once the "applications" are created, it's more a matter of maintenance and keeping things fresh.

It's usually better to outsource development because you can bring in an app development team that is already familiar with each other's individual talents, works fluidly together, and is familiar with a variety of companies and goals. They're more likely to keep up with trends and best practices as well, simply because they have to keep their skills sharp to continue working on the development and launch of new projects. This means they'll be more efficient, and you'll likely receive a better product overall.

Chapter 18

Website Hosting - Your Weakest Digital Marketing Link!

Have you ever gone to a website to place an order or read something and then... nothing? You can only see a few elements on the page, and the content you wanted to view isn't loading? If you're like most people, you'll only wait a few seconds and then leave the page. Maybe you'll return to your search results and pick another option or perhaps end your search altogether at this point.

This scenario is more common than you might think. The likelihood of someone leaving a webpage without taking any action, also referred to as a bounce, increases by 32 percent when a page takes three seconds to load versus one second[i]. The probability of a bounce increases by 90 percent when comparing a five-second load time to a one-second load. In other words, your business website only has a three-second window to load and interest a visitor. That may not be a concern initially, but the average website takes 15 seconds to load. If you're average, you're losing valuable traffic you've worked hard to attract.

There are many causes for slow loads, but website hosting issues are a common culprit. Poor website hosting services can cause lots of other issues as well.

What is Website Hosting?

Websites look like one cohesive unit on the surface, but they're really made up of many individual files. Some files contain coding and tell a browser how something looks or behaves. Media files, like images, are another example. When you visit a website, your browser looks at all these files and then displays the page they describe.

Similar to how your computer stores all your files, such as word processing documents and photos, a server stores the files for each website and makes them publicly available, so anyone with an internet connection can view the website.

Types of Website Hosting

Who owns and maintains the server with all your website files is up to you. Some companies host their own websites. Others outsource it to a web hosting service provider. In these cases, hosting may be offered as a standalone service or bundled with things like a domain name, email, and website builder. As you explore your options, you'll also hear terms like shared, dedicated, VPS, and cloud used.

Self-Hosted

When you host your own website, you can set up the hosting environment any way you want. If you are tech-savvy, you may be able to save money with this option, but it often costs more and can be problematic because you're ultimately responsible for setting up the server, ensuring all the hardware and software are maintained, as well as securing it.

Shared

Shared hosting through a hosting service provider means your website shares a server with other websites. It's typically the most cost-effective website hosting option, but it also means all resources are shared with the other sites. For example, when one website attracts a large amount of traffic, it can slow the traffic to other sites on the same server.

Dedicated

Dedicated website hosting, sometimes referred to as managed hosting, refers to having a server that's rented exclusively to your business by a hosting service provider. It's more expensive than shared hosting, but you're not sharing resources with other websites. That means your site won't be impacted by traffic to other sites.

VPS

VPS is short for a virtual private server. It's also referred to as a virtual dedicated server or VPS. This type of arrangement with a hosting service provider means your data is stored alongside other websites, but when bots and browsers visit your site, they think it's a dedicated server. It's also compartmentalized, so it behaves more like dedicated hosting. As a result, your site won't be impacted by large traffic spikes to another website. Think of it more as a hybrid between dedicated and shared. It won't be as expensive as dedicated but offers benefits shared hosting doesn't.

Cloud

Cloud hosting is one of the newer terms to hit the market. It refers to having your data hosted by a network of dedicated computers in the cloud by a hosting service provider. It opens doors for companies that have lots of data, run resource-intensive applications, or cannot afford to have any downtime, but it's the most expensive of the options listed here, outside of self-hosted, which is wholly dependent on your chosen configurations.

Bad Website Hosting Can Kill Your Digital Marketing Efforts

Before you decide how to host your website, consider the consequences of choosing the wrong hosting option for your needs.

Slow Load Times

Because search engines see high bounce rates and slow loads as a signal that the site isn't delivering on user expectations, they can rank slow sites lower in search results because of this.

Being on a shared website hosting plan will naturally impact load speed from time to time, even when a website hosting provider balances the websites sharing a server carefully. However, not all providers worry about balance, and the amount of traffic is only one factor that influences speed, so self-hosted websites can be quite slow too.

Downtime

All website hosting providers rely on real-world hardware and software. Even if you're hosting in the cloud, there are physical servers somewhere that host your data. They need to be maintained and updated just like your office or home computer does.

A hosting company can't promise 100 percent uptime for this reason. However, the best hosting companies will put measures in place that ensure your uptime is maximized and will typically boast an uptime rate of 99 percent or more. To get similar results while keeping your hosting in-house, you'd need to have around-the-clock employee coverage.

Downtime impacts your site in many ways. Naturally, people can't access your site when it's down. That puts an immediate halt to your traffic. It can also affect traffic over time, as people stop depending on your site as a source of information or help. Search engines notice when your site is down and may drop your rankings as your site is seen as unreliable.

Scalability

It's important to think of both short-term and long-term scalability when it comes to website hosting. For example, some sites have slowdowns when lots of traffic hits or set limits to avoid resource allocation issues. That might not be a problem in most cases, but what if your business runs a successful email campaign and you get a large increase in traffic or content you've published goes viral? You're undermining your efforts if they can't get through to your website or leave because your site speeds are throttled.

Equally, long-term scalability matters too. If your site can't handle your future traffic, can't handle upgrades, or you're unable to migrate your data to a new host and server, your website host can hinder business growth. If you're self-hosting, you can scale on-demand, but you'll need to be ready to pay for any additional hardware or software needs as well as labor expenses.

Error Monitoring

Well-maintained websites are constantly evolving. You'll update plugins and add-ons, update pages, remove old pages, and so forth. Browsers are constantly evolving and updating their coding too, which can change how your site displays and functions. You must be on top of these changes to ensure your visitors have a good experience.

Error monitoring is a part of that. Some web hosting companies monitor for you or at least make it easy to install code and plugins that handle monitoring. Others, especially the type that bundles website builders with hosting, generally don't offer error monitoring and can sometimes make it difficult to leverage third-party applications. If you're self-hosting, you're wholly responsible for setting up all error monitoring tools, plus ensuring someone is monitoring them and taking action if there are issues.

Location

It may go without saying, but the farther your server is from the person visiting your website, the longer it takes data to travel and the longer it takes your site and features to load. Therefore, it's beneficial to have your website hosted near your customer base for that reason alone.

However, some search engines also look at your server's location to determine ranking. "The server location is often physically near your users and can be a signal about your site's intended audience," according to Google Search Central. The search engine notes it uses this info to determine a target locale, so it can impact who sees your website or page as well, though it doesn't consider location a definitive signal.

Because of this, self-hosting may not be ideal if your server is not geographically close to your audience or if you plan to expand. You'll also want to discuss server locations if you're working with a hosting provider.

Messy Coding

The need for clean coding is often overlooked. Think of how you might read a book, then imagine you reach a line in which you're told you must read a paragraph in another book before moving forward. If it only happens once or twice, it won't slow you down too much, but if it happens repeatedly, or if the secondary books send you to other sources to read before moving forward, you're going to slow down considerably. The same thing happens with websites.

WordPress sites and those with similar frameworks can sometimes behave this way. However, website hosting companies may inject their own code too. This is seen more often when the host also provides a website builder. You may have issues with messy coding if you're self-hosting and your IT professional is overwhelmed or inexperienced. It tends to happen more often when your in-house role has more turnover too. Using the book example again, it can be like a choose your own adventure book, only each chapter has a different author. Sometimes the storylines line up, but you'll probably wind up with awkward jumps and inconsistencies unless someone invests the time to edit it all in the end.

Security and Backups

Webmasters are often cautioned about the importance of updating plugins to reduce security risks, but it's rarely mentioned that hosting companies have similar risks. Paulos Yibelo, a self-proclaimed "bug hunter" (AKA white-hat hacker), discovered vulnerabilities in five well-known hosting providers a few years back[ii]. The issues meant that other hackers could target around seven million domains, often taking over a user's full account. If companies that specialize in web hosting can have security issues like this, it's easy to see how a standalone company without their resources that's self-hosting might fare.

It can take businesses years and hundreds of thousands of dollars to recover from a cyberattack. Search engines are also wary of ranking sites that have been compromised in the past as well. But, even small-scale attacks or corrupt data can derail a company's online footprint without a good backup. Some hosting companies keep them for you and offer guarantees, while others leave it to you to find a solution. If you're self-hosted, it's entirely your responsibility to manage all these risks.

Customer Service

Although the level of service you receive from your website hosting company may not impact your digital marketing, many of the above concerns can be addressed through quality customer service, assistance when you need it, and professional insights when you're not sure which services are right for your needs.

Unfortunately, many hosting providers fall short in this department. Some are unhelpful or slow to respond. Others don't have live support options at all. Customer service is a big deal when your hard-earned SEO ranking and reputation are on the line.

Companies that self-host run into a similar issue. You not only need a team of people who can provide around-the-clock coverage, but the people you hire must be knowledgeable in all the areas covered here.

In-House vs Outsourced Website Hosting

Although self-hosting is versatile, it's not worth the headache and additional complications for most businesses. You'll have a faster, more stable, securer website, and will generally save money if you outsource to a website hosting provider.

Choosing a Good Outsourced Provider

The right website hosting provider and plan will vary based on your company's needs. Use the following questions to gauge the quality of any hosting providers you're considering.

- Can the hosting provider scale with my needs?
- How fast will my site load?
- What kind of uptime does the company guarantee?
- Will the hosting provider help keep my site and data secure?
- Will the provider enable me to ensure my site is running optimally?
- Will the location of my server impact my visitors and SEO positively?
- Who will help me and how will they help if I have an issue?

[i] Daniel An. "Find out how you stack up to new industry benchmarks for mobile page speed." Google. https://bit.ly/dmo-18-i

 [ii] Zack Whittaker. "Some of the biggest web hosting sites were vulnerable to simple account takeover hacks." TechCrunch. https://bit.ly/dmo-18-ii

Chapter 19

Should You Outsource Video Production or Keep it In-House?

Videos keep visitors on a page longer, increase engagement, and can boost the likelihood of a purchase by 64 percent[i]. It's no wonder that nearly nine in ten businesses incorporate them in their digital marketing strategies.

However, achieving strong video marketing results requires having a professional on board, which means you'll either need to hire someone in-house or outsource the role. We'll explore what both scenarios look like in this chapter.

The Role of Video Production

Video production tools are now a dime a dozen. You can use free online editors and whip up something simple in under an hour, even if you have no previous video creation skills.

The more you're willing to spend on a video editing or production tool, the more features you can unlock, and the more polished your finished piece will look. But, there's a lot more involved in being a good producer than simply finding the right tools and knowing how to use them.

For starters, producers must be familiar with the primary goal of the clip—to generate awareness, create engagement, or educate the audience. They need to have a firm grasp on the audience and what they'll respond to, plus be able to tailor the video content to the channel in which it's being distributed.

For example, people watching a video on a Facebook feed are going to be more engaged if it's short and they can tell what's happening without sound. On a channel like YouTube, extended footage with sound is better. There are also considerations like the type of video—will you be filming real people or using animation?

A strong video producer explores all these areas and more to identify what will work best, blend the strategy with your branding and key messages, and monitor the results to ensure you're getting the mileage you deserve.

A few steps involved in the production process include:

- Creating a video brief
- Scriptwriting
- Storyboarding
- Scouting locations (if filming)
- Production
- Adding animations, motion graphics, music, and effects
- Final editing

Core Competencies and Resources

Video production is multifaceted. To do it right, a professional needs a variety of skills and tools.

Effective video production professionals have a diverse skill set.

Some of the skills required in video production include:

- Ability to write clear, concise scripts (or bring your writer in on this)
- An understanding of your branding and ability to consistently apply your standards
- An understanding of analytics and the ability to adapt an approach to improve results (should work closely with your analytics team and digital marketing manager)
- Familiarity with various channels such as email marketing, social media marketing channels, and best practices on each (YouTube videos, Facebook, Instagram, TikTok)
- An understanding of SEO and web markups

- Communication, both with the team and with the external audience

Video production professionals should know how to work with various tools.

Some of the most common tools leveraged include:

- Production tools
- Editing tools
- Filming equipment (cameras, microphones, lights, props)
- Collaboration software
- Analytics tracking

Time investments will vary by project.

The time involved will vary greatly depending on the video length, the number of videos you release, and the style of the videos. Skill, access to tools, and other factors will impact the time investment as well. All steps considered, it typically takes a professional team a minimum of two weeks to work through the process of creating a one or two-minute video. However, it's not uncommon for a more advanced production to take two months or more.

While you can, in theory, pass this task off to another member of your video content marketing team and give them a window of time to produce something, it won't have the same polish or produce the same results as one that specialists create in the video production process who have the time and tools necessary to do the job right.

Identifying Success in Video Production

As discussed, there are three primary reasons businesses create videos: brand awareness, engagement, and education. The KPIs will vary depending on your overall goals.

Use KPIs to measure success.

- Views
- Plays
- View-through or play-through Rate
- Click-through rate
- Watch time
- Impressions
- Channel subscribers

- Unique viewers/ users
- Likes/ shares
- Conversion rate

Making the Final Decision

As you can see, the production of marketing videos is rarely handled by a single person. To do it well, a team of individuals, each with unique skills, come together to create a quality piece. Moreover, each duty typically requires different tools.

It can be cost-prohibitive for an organization to purchase everything necessary, especially if the in-house team won't be producing several videos per week. With that in mind, it's usually better to outsource your video marketing. You'll likely save money overall and get better results through outsourced video marketing services.

[i] Adam Hayes. "What Video Marketers Should Know, According to Wyzowl Research." HubSpot. https://bit.ly/dmo-19-i

Chapter 20

Should You Outsource Digital Marketing Analytics or Keep it In-House?

Believe it or not, the number of businesses that identify as being data-driven is declining, down more than six percent in just a few years[i]. While this is disappointing to hear, it does mean that those who create a culture of data within their businesses stand to gain a major competitive edge.

As someone who Google once retained to educate their Partners, I'm a big believer in the power of digital marketing analytics. Ensuring that the companies I work with effectively leverage the data at their disposal is one of the many things I address now as a business and digital marketing consultant, and something you'll want to include in your digital marketing strategy too.

In this chapter, I'll cover some of the things I take into consideration when deciding whether it's best for a company to outsource this crucial role, so it's easier for you to make an informed decision for your company.

The Role of a Digital Marketing Analyst

A digital marketing analyst uses data to identify the health of digital marketing campaigns. You'll get an in-depth look at some of the top metrics in the next chapter. For now, you can think of it as data that relates to whether you're attracting the right kind of traffic and if your visitors are taking the actions you want them to take.

Because of this, the analyst should be present before kicking off a campaign. That way, they can help you determine which KPIs are best to measure your success and track throughout the campaign. They'll also make sure your analytics program is set up correctly to ensure meaningful data is captured. They'll monitor the results of campaigns and make recommendations based on their expertise to boost your marketing team's success and capabilities too.

In some cases, your digital marketing analyst will take on additional digital marketing management and project management duties as well, such as identifying who your customers are, what types of things they'll purchase, and how much they'll pay.

Core Competencies and Resources

Effective analysts don't just need to know how to read data. They must know what tools to leverage to capture the data they require, how to implement those tools, how to interpret the data captured, and then how to turn the data into actionable steps.

For example, even an entry-level analyst should be able to tell when visitors to one of your landing pages leaves too soon based on time-on-page metrics and bounce rates. A stronger analyst, however, will recognize the page is underperforming and find out why. They may look at other landing pages that are performing well to see if there's a difference that might be diminishing results. They might look at the ad that's bringing visitors to the page to see if there's a disconnect in the language being used when a person jumps from the ad to the page. They may look at the traffic you're attracting to identify if you're reaching the right people. They may also install additional tools, such as heat maps and screen recorders, to see what's happening when people land on the page.

Effective digital marketing analysts have a diverse skill set.

A few skills to look for include:

- An understanding of your brand
- An understanding of your market and audience(s)
- An understanding of the company's objectives
- Data analysis

- Communication
- Comfortable with AI and automation

Analysts should know how to work with various tools.

Historically, Google Analytics was the golden standard of web analytics. It's still incredibly powerful, but particularly as organizations move to the enterprise level, additional tools are brought in to examine data at a deeper level. As there are literally thousands of tools available, broad categories of tool types are outlined below.

- Cross-channel attribution (tracking where a conversion initially came from)
- Customer segmentation (dividing your audience into subgroups or finding new audiences)
- Customer journey (follow individual customers from their first interaction through conversion)
- Competitive analysis (evaluate the strengths and weaknesses of your competitors)
- And more

Setup and maintenance times will vary.

Getting the right tools in place makes a huge difference in the amount of time needed for your marketing operations. Tasks like data wrangling, integration, and formatting each take up more time than the actual analysis for a typical marketing analyst[ii]. With that in mind, a smaller company may not need a full-time employee for digital marketing analytics, but you'll need one or more full-time analytics pros as you grow.

Identifying Success in Digital Marketing Analytics

Your analyst is the one providing you with metrics on all your other KPIs, so it can be a bit difficult to measure the success of these professionals. But rest assured, you can still measure their success, just not necessarily using the same types of KPIs you'd use in other areas.

Use KPIs to measure success.

- Attentiveness to regular reporting
- Number of solutions the pro is involved in
- Team use of insights provided

- Comprehensive plans to acquire new data or deploy new analytics applications
- Alignment of data initiatives with corporate strategy and business priorities

Making the Final Decision

Many people will suggest third-party outsourcing because a lot goes into getting good analytical insights, and it's not a core competency for most organizations. I tend to disagree with this philosophy simply because your analytics professional(s) must align with the business and all its initiatives.

Unless your digital marketing analyst is kept in-house, it's very difficult to have a pulse on what's happening within the company. Yes, you will need to find someone who is well-qualified and trustworthy, and you will need to invest in good tools to ensure the job can be done well, but when you have these things in place, you'll get the information you need to be able to build marketing strategies to surpass the nearly 70 percent of businesses that are not data-driven.

[i] Randy Bean. "Companies Are Failing in Their Efforts to Become Data-Driven." Harvard Business Review. https://bit.ly/dmo-20-i

[ii] Chris Pemberton. "Key Findings From Gartner Marketing Analytics Survey." Gartner. https://bit.ly/dmo-20-ii

Chapter 21

Metrics to Measure Your Marketing Success

You may have noticed that, as we touched on each marketing role, I listed KPIs to help you gauge the success of the role or effectiveness of the person performing those duties. Everything your marketing team does should be measurable. The same extends to your digital marketing as a whole.

Oftentimes, businesses use KPIs such as how much it costs to acquire a new customer or lead, how many new leads any given campaign draws, or sales revenue generated. These are excellent metrics to track. But, what if you have unique goals or simply have a gnawing feeling that you could be doing better and aren't sure what will help you improve?

In this chapter, you'll get a quick overview of some of the most common metrics used to measure marketing success and a few more that businesses commonly overlook. Although it's not intended to be a definitive guide to digital marketing metrics, as whole books can be devoted to the topic, it will help you begin with a data-driven mindset and provide some background on things to watch.

Sales Revenue Generated by Marketing

Perhaps the most fundamental measurement of your marketing success is how much revenue your marketing strategy generates for your business. Bear in mind that this is not the end-all, as many valuable marketing benefits aren't represented in revenue. Brand awareness, for example, is a big one. Even still, you should have the processes in place to ensure you can measure the revenue your marketing is creating for your organization so you can funnel your investments into what's really driving the business forward.

As a business consultant, this is an area I concentrate on. Digital marketing is a fantastic revenue grower, but you need to have an effective strategy and measure what really works for your organization to receive the benefits.

Return on Marketing Investment (ROMI)

ROMI, also known as ROI, goes hand-in-hand with revenue. It's great if your marketing campaigns result in one million in sales, but if those sales cost two million to generate, it's obviously not a good situation. However, as with revenue, it's not the whole picture of success. Many things that will contribute to overall growth that won't necessarily be reflected in ROMI, and there are times when you have to spend a bit more upfront to develop long-term customers. Nevertheless, here is a simple method to calculate Return on Marketing Investment (ROMI):

Marketing Generated Revenue / Marketing Spend = ROMI

Cost Per Lead

No matter how you reach people, there will always be a dollar amount it takes to attract each business lead. This is true whether you're using traditional channels, such as print and radio, or digital marketing channels. Knowing the cost per lead allows you to budget more effectively and put your investments toward the activities that are producing the best results.

Inbound Marketing Lead Expenses

It's easy to look at the cost-per-click (CPC), cost per acquisition (CPA), or customer acquisition cost (CAC) provided by your analytical software (such as Google Analytics), but it's only a portion of the actual expenses involved in attracting a new lead. Include all overhead costs, software, technology, and labor to get a clearer picture.

Outbound Marketing Lead Expenses

Outbound campaigns have similar expenses too. Consider your overhead, labor, distribution, and advertising costs in your calculations.

Customer Lifetime Value

The calculation for customer lifetime value (CLV) will vary somewhat based on your business model. Oftentimes, it's the product of an average sale multiplied by the average number of purchases a customer makes in a year and the average retention time. In these cases, you may be able to increase CLV by reaching out to existing customers to discuss additional products.

Other business models involve subscriptions. In these cases, your CLV is the product of monthly subscription times the average retention rate. CLV can be boosted through customer loyalty programs and upgrading to the next tier of service.

Regardless of the methodology and business model, happy customers refer other customers to you, so this should be factored into your CLV calculations as well.

Traffic-to-Lead Ratio

Traffic is a KPI that almost everyone tracks. It's simple, easy, and virtually any platform you might use will provide you with the metric. The problem is that all the website traffic in the world won't help if those visitors don't eventually take action or if your website has a high bounce rate. Things like signing up for your newsletter or downloading a whitepaper, make these visitors new leads, provided you have a system in place to capture their information. Phone calls, online contact forms, emails, live chat, and social media messaging are common methods used to capture leads.

A/B testing is a good way to improve your traffic-to-lead ratio. Simply make small tweaks to your page to see if it improves the conversion rate. Equally, you can watch your conversions alongside your traffic. If traffic climbs and conversions don't, it usually means there's a disconnect between what the visitor expects to find and what he does. It can also signify that there's something off with the offer you're presenting. A/B testing will help you get to the bottom of it as well.

When you do A/B testing, only change up one element at a time, so it's easy to identify which change people responded to. For example, on your A variant, you might offer guests a 25 percent discount, while on your B variant, you might offer guests something free. Other individual elements to experiment with are colors, verbiage, headings, length, and the type of social proof displayed.

Lead Progress Ratios

There are three stages for leads you'll want to measure (Classify, Qualify, and Solidify); sales classified leads (Leads), sales qualified leads (Prospects), and sales solidified leads (Opportunities). The lead progress ratios will differ for each stage. Monitoring the numbers can help you identify if your sales team is getting the right leads from the marketing team, if the sales team is attending to these leads at the right time, and whether the sales team is doing an adequate job of advancing these leads to become customers.

Sales Classified Leads (Leads)

A sales-classified-lead (Lead) is someone who has given signs they're interested in what you offer or have been selected or acquired as a minimum viable contact (MVC) for discussing business with but aren't ready to purchase yet. Robust tracking systems can measure things like website engagement, the number of visits, and other metrics to provide you with a list of potential customers. People who make their way onto one of these lists will typically need a little more TLC to carry them through the sales funnel until they close as customers, so they shouldn't be treated the same as those who are ready to take action. This stage is extremely essential to filter out irrelevant inquiries (such as those from vendors or jobseekers) from real Leads. Relevant metric: Cost-Per-Lead.

Sales Qualified Leads (Prospects)

A sales-qualified-lead, or SQL, (Prospect) is someone who has outright initiated the buying process with specific requirements, or you have selected them proactively as a potential client, AND they meet your qualification criteria. Perhaps they requested a consultation, analysis of their requirements, etc. These people are usually a lot easier to move forward in the sales process compared to marketing qualified leads (MQL) because they've done some research and/or meet your minimum qualification criteria. Relevant metric: Cost-Per-Prospect.

Sales Solidified Leads (Opportunities)

A sales-solidified-lead (Opportunity) is someone who is prepared to do business with you, as long as they are satisfied with your offer and other requirements they may have. Perhaps they requested a proposal or asked for a price estimate (the magical question: How Much?). These people are much more advanced in the sales cycle and will be ready to take action if the final offer matches their expectations. Relevant metric: Cost-Per-Opportunity.

Landing Page Conversion Rates

It may not need to be said, but anytime you're advertising or giving people a special offer, that offer deserves its own landing page. That means people who click are sent to a page created expressly for their needs and designed to convert them or carry them through your funnel. They should never be sent to a standard webpage or your homepage.

Furthermore, the effectiveness of your landing page should be tracked, just like you track your traffic-to-lead ratio. If you're already following best practices on your landing page and they're not becoming leads, or you simply want to ensure you're using the most effective landing pages possible, do A/B testing.

Organic Traffic

Organic search traffic drives 51 percent of traffic to average B2B and B2C sites[i], though the amount varies by industry. For example, business services usually get 73 percent of their direct visitors. Retail sits on the other end of the spectrum at little more than 40 percent. If your organization doesn't measure up to industry standards, it's time to explore what's happening with your SEO (Search Engine Optimization) and whether you're leveraging the right keyword strategy to optimize your search engine rankings and keyword rankings. Doing so means you're getting optimal returns for unpaid campaigns and often minimizing your marketing expenses overall.

Social Media Metrics

Monitoring social media can seem a bit like opening Pandora's Box. You've got followers/fans, impressions, clicks, engagement, shares, comments, and more for every single social media platform you're on, such as Facebook, Twitter, and LinkedIn. Optimizing your social media campaigns is complex, but as a baseline, you should be tracking how much traffic you're getting from each platform and your conversion rate for each platform. Doing so will make it easier to pinpoint which ones deserve resource investments and which ones you can let go of.

Inbound Link Performance

Technically speaking, links from social media count as inbound links to your site, but websites that perform best have a large portfolio of inbound links from other reputable sites as well. If article placement or press releases are part of your strategy, you may be able to get stats from these sources or Google Analytics to indicate which sources are performing. However, you'll likely have an easier time tracking the performance of specific campaigns using UTM (Urchin Tracking Module) links. These specialized links are readable by Google and other marketing platforms and contain tracking codes that make it easy to identify traffic sources.

Mobile Data

Google prioritizes indexing a mobile version of a page over the desktop version[ii]. This is because 94 percent of people with smartphones use them to monitor and search for local information, and 77 percent of mobile searches occur at home or work, even though most people have desktop computers in these locations.

Your audience may be slightly different, especially if it focuses on the B2B niche. Even still, mobile traffic matters. Check into your analytics to see how much traffic comes from mobile sources and how user behavior differs from your desktop website visitors. Do you see more bounces or fewer conversions? It could be that your mobile experience is not up to par. Try to pinpoint what's going wrong and adapt your site to meet the needs of mobile visitors better.

Monitor What Matters Most to You and Your Company

Some of the metrics outlined in this chapter, such as mobile data and sales revenue generated by marketing, are universal. Virtually all companies will want to keep an eye on them from the start. Other metrics, such as lifetime value and landing page conversion rates, may not come into play until your business or marketing strategy is more established. This is one of the reasons it's a good idea to keep your analytics professional in-house. They will help make sure you're tracking metrics that align with your business and digital marketing goals and be an invaluable resource that helps ensure you're always getting top ROMI.

[i] Amy Gesenhues. "Study: Organic Search Drives 51% Of Traffic, Social Only 5%." Search Engine Land. https://bit.ly/dmo-21-i

[ii] Google. "Mobile-first indexing best practices." Google. https://bit.ly/dmo-21-ii

Chapter 22

Advantages of Digital Marketing Outsourcing

Y ou've now walked through various digital marketing initiatives and priorities, the roles you'll need to fill, how to fill them, the tools your team needs, and how to measure your success. That's quite a bit to learn in such a short period of time!

One of the key points, as we explored in various roles, is whether it makes sense to outsource each one. Digital marketing outsourcing is not an all-or-nothing deal. It's best when paired with in-house talent. You get the best of all worlds when you approach it with this methodology.

However, no resource on digital marketing outsourcing would be complete without a balanced look at the advantages and disadvantages of the strategy. Let's dig into the advantages first.

Experience

It's often said that it takes 10,000 hours or ten years of deliberate practice to become an expert. Popularized by Malcolm Gladwell in "Outliers[i]," the concept draws on examples throughout history—from composers to artists—and indicates few people create publicly known works until they've honed their craft for at least a decade.

That's who you want on your digital marketing team too. However, experienced professionals are in short supply. A typical digital marketing manager, for example, has only five years of experience or less[ii]. It's challenging to build a quality digital marketing team when the lion's share of the talent pool doesn't have the experience you need. Because outsourced digital marketing professionals tend to work on multiple projects at once, it's much easier to find someone who has the experience you need.

Industry Expertise

Industry expertise is just as important as experience. You need to work with marketing professionals who understand your brand, challenges, and customers. It's hard enough to find someone with experience due to the talent shortage but finding someone who knows your industry on top of it, let alone building an entire team of people like this, is close to impossible in some niches. Outsourcing widens the talent pool, so it's easier to create your dream team.

Trends and Current Knowledge

It's estimated that Google changes its search algorithm around 500 to 600 times each year[iii]. This is only one facet of one role. While an in-house professional can certainly read articles and keep a pulse on what's happening in their area of expertise, their information is wholly limited to how each change impacted your business and the limited number of steps they took to account for it.

When you outsource, your team is working on a multitude of projects and interacting with other professionals outside your business more. That means they'll know which strategies are performing for businesses today and how various approaches impact the effectiveness of campaigns. It's like having the knowledge of a small army at your disposal.

Performance

When you have a team of industry specialists putting their experience and the latest trends to work for your brand, your marketing campaigns perform better. They'll also monitor your metrics more and continuously improve the results.

Continuity

Nearly 60 percent of chief marketing officers have been in their position for three years or less[iv]. Challenges abound, from misunderstandings about what the role entails to limited decision-making abilities. This constant changing of the guards impacts everything, from the strategies in play to branding and team morale. By outsourcing digital marketing, you can keep key players in place longer.

Furthermore, your campaign rollouts are more consistent, as you're no longer balancing vacations and sick days with releases. Instead, your digital marketing outsourcing provider ensures rollouts happen on schedule.

Cost Reduction

Wages and salaries only account for about two-thirds of employee compensation[v] paid out by employers. The remainder goes to benefits. Because outsourced talent does not typically receive benefit packages, labor expenses reduce considerably. As explored earlier, outsourced talent generally provides their own supplies and working space too. Plus, much of your team can work on-demand rather than having an ongoing salary, which brings the average cost down. Outsourcing is generally far more cost-effective for these reasons.

ROI

Analytics is important in digital marketing. First, data is leveraged to help refine campaigns and improve them over time, so return on investment climbs as your team turns up the dials on what's working for your audience. Secondly, outsourced marketing teams often use analytics to demonstrate the growth they're producing for the companies they serve.

When teams have high analytics usage rates, their marketing budgets are a whopping 70 percent higher than their counterparts[vi]. Undoubtedly, companies see the ROI they're receiving and are eager to amplify the results.

Focus

The average small business owner works at least 50 hours per week, with 25 percent clocking at least 60[vii]. Startup employees are not immune, often expected to work 50-60 hours each week[viii]. While there's something to be said for grit and cross-training, there are only so many hours in a day and dollars available to your company. Digital marketing outsourcing frees you and your team to focus on core functions of your business and unlocks resources being tied up in inefficient or ineffective processes.

Maximize the Benefits

Remember, you don't need to outsource all your digital marketing to receive these benefits. You'll get the best results when you selectively outsource specific roles. Refer back to the digital marketing tree and build out your strategy and team one piece at a time.

[i] Malcolm Gladwell. Outliers: The Story of Success. (New York, New York: Little, Brown and Company).

[ii] PayScale. "Average Digital Marketing Manager Salary." PayScale. https://bit.ly/dmo-22-ii

[iii] Search Engine Land. (N.D.). "Google SEO news: Google algorithm updates." Search Engine Land. https://bit.ly/dmo-22-3

[iv] Kimberly Whitler. "Why CMOs Never Last." https://bit.ly/dmo-22-iv

[v] Bureau of Labor Statistics. "Employer Costs for Employee Compensation." U.S. Department of Labor. https://bit.ly/dmo-22-v

 [vi] Deloitte. "Marketing Budgets Vary by Industry." Deloitte. https://bit.ly/dmo-22-6

 [vii] Ted Callahan. "Business Owners Work Twice as Much as Employees, Survey Finds." Inc. https://bit.ly/dmo-22-7

 [viii] Julie Bort. "The unwritten rules of working at a startup that no one likes to talk about." https://bit.ly/dmo-22-viii

Chapter 23

Disadvantages of Digital Marketing Outsourcing

As we explored the roles earlier, I identified some points where the disadvantages of outsourcing a particular role may outweigh the potential benefits. The contrast was necessary to help you think more critically about the individual roles and evaluate your options as I do. However, there are some disadvantages or pitfalls that can exist across the board. I'll touch on these concerns in this chapter and provide a few pointers on how to avoid them.

Less Company and Culture Exposure

One of the best things about keeping your marketing in-house is that the team gets to know your business and customers inside and out. Because freelancers may interact with your business infrequently and agencies split their time between projects, they don't usually develop the kind of bond with your company that an insider would. Allow me to provide a few examples.

Scenario 1

A freelancer handles your analytics for you. They're responsible for gathering and presenting data. Having an insider who's always available so you can improve results dramatically, but your analytics professional may be able to deliver results regardless if they invest time and get to know your business.

Scenario 2

You run a company that makes specialized CRM and billing software for accountants. An agency manages your PPC. Because the agency doesn't know your company or customers well, they don't realize that a search for "accounting software" is usually a business looking to purchase software they can use versus an accountant looking for software their firm can use. In the end, you wind up needlessly spending thousands of dollars marketing to the wrong audience. This isn't necessarily an issue of in-house vs. outsourcing. Outsourced talent can perform the job, but you need someone with industry knowledge.

Scenario 3

A freelancer manages your social media and logs in to find a customer complaining about a product issue and a prospective customer asking about product features. Not having insider information, the freelancer either gives erroneous answers or kicks the questions back to you for a reply. Meanwhile, tensions mount as your social media queries wait. It's technically possible to find a freelancer who can perform well, but because they're removed from your company, you're usually better off keeping the role in-house.

Brand Consistency May be Lacking

Ever heard the phrase "too many cooks in the kitchen?" That can happen with your digital marketing too. Even when two people are given the exact same guidelines, they can produce radically different things. Your brand voice may sound different from one person to the next, colors may be different, shapes won't match... the list goes on.

Addressing Consistency

To keep branding consistent, you either need to keep certain roles in-house or provide creatives with a detailed style guide, templates, and other materials. Your results will be even better if your team collaborates and has dedicated asset sharing.

Availability and Schedules

The moment you start telling freelancers or agencies when they have to work, they stop being outsourced talent and become employees. In many cases, that may mean you're responsible for offering them the same benefits as employees, and employee taxes start to apply. It can hurt the relationship too.

There will, however, inevitably be times you need work completed urgently or simply want to touch base with your team when it's convenient for you. Unfortunately, it's not as simple as stopping by someone's desk when you're outsourcing.

Addressing Availability

You can get around this by planning workloads, tasks, and meetings ahead of time. Using a good project management tool will help greatly with this. In addition, if you develop strong relationships with your extended team, they may volunteer to jump in for the occasional unexpected need too.

Cost Management

Unexpected and hidden charges are one of the biggest disadvantages of outsourcing digital marketing. This can happen for a variety of reasons.

Failure to Discuss Limits

It can be uncomfortable to discuss money and hours worked, but it's essential to understand how much you'll spend on tasks before your talent starts work.

Miscommunication

Sometimes, business owners and talent have different ideas about what it takes to complete a project.

Scope Creep

Maybe you started off thinking you wanted a website and then realized you wanted it optimized midway too, only to find that's an extra charge. Or, maybe you asked for a ten-page site but then realized the site needed special functionality.

Intentional Slowness

Unfortunately, some hourly talent will intentionally work slowly to increase their billable hours. This can happen with in-house talent too, though.

Upcharges

Particularly with agencies and specialty firms, you may find there are surprise upcharges. For example, you might look at sample blogs on a website and see the company is charging a low price for content, only to submit an order and find out there are additional charges if you want a subject matter expert, longer copy, editing, optimization, and so forth.

Addressing Cost Management

Regardless of who you're outsourcing to, the only way to manage these issues is to have your agreement in writing, develop good relationships with talent, monitor results, and take corrective action if your extended team isn't delivering on your cost expectations.

Protecting Proprietary Data

One of the most worrisome disadvantages of outsourcing digital marketing is the potential security risk. It's hard to know if you have the same level of loyalty as you do with in-house employees, and there will be times your team needs access to things like pre-market product info, customer data, and company numbers.

Addressing Proprietary Data

The reality is that data issues can creep up with in-house talent too. Errors may be made, or disgruntled employees may intentionally share info. Protecting proprietary data is handled much the same either way. Limit data sharing only to those who need to know. Have the team sign NDAs and similar agreements. When you're sharing sensitive data, always remind people that it's not public knowledge and needs to be kept confidential.

Disadvantages Can Often Be Avoided

There are times, as is the case with social media, when it's generally best to retain in-house talent. However, many roles can go either way or are better served by outsourced talent even though there are potential drawbacks. As you begin strategizing, defining roles, and hiring, refer back to this chapter to ensure you're addressing the concerns outlined here, so you can avoid any pitfalls from the start.

Chapter 24

7 Essential Traits of a Marketing Strategist

As you move into more advanced techniques and accelerate your digital marketing, you'll need to onboard someone with more tactical and leadership abilities. You'll need a digital marketing strategist.

Unlike your digital marketing manager, who oversees daily activities and ensures campaigns and initiatives are performing, the strategist has a long-term vision and brings marketing into alignment with business objectives. Through their insights and methodology, your digital marketing produces stronger results and better ROMI. It becomes the kind of department that easily earns its 70 percent higher budget because company leadership sees the numbers and the value their initiatives bring to the business.

This isn't an ordinary role in which you can gauge qualifications with a list of hard skills as you might with some of the others we've explored. Instead, you need to know how this person operates. The traits outlined in this chapter will make it easier for you to identify the right person for the role.

1. Strong Business Acumen

Strong business acumen goes beyond understanding the world of business. It's about combining one's knowledge and experience with situational awareness and making strategic decisions that benefit the business as a whole in the long run. Virtually every decision your strategist makes should tie back to this concept, from which personas to target to what technology to adopt and when to roll out specific initiatives.

2. Ability to Turn Analytics into Action

Earlier, we discussed how marketing teams with high analytics usage rates have 70 percent higher budgets than their counterparts[i], but what does the inverse look like? CMO surveys reveal just 29 percent of businesses have invested in advanced measurement techniques and analytics[ii]. They also note that less than two-thirds can link digital marketing returns to business outcomes such as profit.

That's not to say what they're doing isn't helping. It might be. The problem is that they cannot prove it. If they can't prove they're contributing to something as clearcut as profitability, how can they know which of their marketing initiatives are producing results? How can they know which areas to put more resources into and which initiatives to drop? How can they know how to improve their results? They can't.

A strong strategist knows which analytics to leverage and what the numbers are telling them, then uses that intel to guide their decisions.

3. ROMI-Focused, But Customer-Centric

We often talk about ROMI and how a good strategist not only ensures their initiatives are returning the investment but also improving that return over time as approaches are finetuned. That still stands. However, it's possible to get top ROMI while performing a disservice to the company and/or customer.

For example, a marketing team can over-promise or mislead customers in their marketing materials. These campaigns may get good ROMI, but what happens when those leads reach the sales department and are found to be unqualified? The business loses money.

Or, let's say the customer purchases based on those marketing materials. They will become disenchanted with the brand and may become detractors who leave bad reviews. Even those who don't purchase may see the marketing materials and lose faith in the brand.

ROMI is important, but it's not just about getting a return. Your strategist must embody the customer-first mentality because each action they take impacts the customer and, thusly, the brand.

4. Inquisitive and Tailored

It's easy for marketers to get ahead of themselves and focus exclusively on immediate gain, profit, and revenue. These things are important. Your strategist should know how to help you achieve your goals in these areas. However, these are not always the end goal for a business. For example, maybe you intend to sell your company within the next year. A great PPC campaign can boost your sales, but it will not increase your overall online presence. Or, maybe a new competitor is diminishing your sales. Running the same campaigns you've always run may not be enough to differentiate your brand and increase your sales.

An experienced strategist will begin with many questions about where you want your company to go and why, then tailor their approach to meet your goals. They'll also revisit the goals regularly and adapt their strategy to suit current conditions and pivots.

5. Speaks the C-Suite Language as a Team Player

Earlier, I mentioned that 60 percent of CMOs have been in their job for three years or less[iii]. There's a somber reason for this. Many, perhaps even most, CMOs don't speak the C-suite language. Little more than half of all businesses say their marketing leaders work collaboratively with the CIO or CTO, and just 40 percent say their CFO is aligned with the company's digital marketing KPIs[iv]. More alarmingly, 80 percent of CEOs say they don't trust or are unimpressed with their CMOs[v]. If digital marketing initiatives are to be successful, there must be collaboration between departments.

The CIO and marketing leaders should be sharing the data they gather and working together to make the most efficient and effective use of the technology and data they have.

A CFO isn't going to award a larger budget to a marketing department if they don't understand how the company is getting that money back.

A CEO is not going to have confidence in a marketing leader if they can't see how their initiatives are driving the company forward and boosting profit.

Sales and product development are the same too. The list goes on.

Unfortunately, marketers often work in silos. They don't always know how to get buy-in from other departments or have the data to demonstrate their worth. These aren't skills many marketers have the opportunity to develop, and is why so many upper-level marketers don't stay in their positions very long. It's also why it's imperative that your digital marketing strategist can.

6. Experience with a Wide Range of Marketing Technology

If you think back to the chapters on project management and password management, you might have noticed I listed about a dozen specific options and then outlined what to look for in case you wanted to evaluate something that didn't make the list. I did the same when outlining some of the tools used in different roles too. This is because what works for one business may not work for the next. Likewise, what works for one professional may not work for another. A strong strategist will have experience with a wide variety of technology so that they can do the same thing for your business across the board.

Bear in mind that about a third of companies don't believe their marketing leaders have a good understanding of the technology roadmap and capabilities they can use to enhance their marketing[vi]. Some of this comes from a lack of experience, as outlined here, but technology is constantly evolving. It also ties back to having a strong relationship with other leaders, especially the CIO/CTO, and a personal belief that lifelong learning is essential.

7. Dream Team Mentality

Better teams produce better results. This is why I advocate for placing an expert in each role you're filling. Your strategist should have this mentality too, and always be building out your marketing dream team.

Choose Your Digital Marketing Strategist Wisely

An effective digital marketing strategist addresses change head-on, brings about a positive change when required, and leads the team in the right direction. When you fill this role with the right person, regardless of how you source the talent, everything else falls into alignment.

 [i] Deloitte. "Marketing Budgets Vary by Industry." Deloitte. https://bit.ly/dmo-24-i

 [ii] Deloitte. "The CMO Survey." Deloitte. https://bit.ly/dmo-24-ii

 [iii] Kimberly Whitler. "Why CMOs Never Last." https://bit.ly/dmo-24-iii

 [iv] Deloitte. "The CMO Survey." Deloitte. https://bit.ly/dmo-24-iv

 [v] Kimberly Whitler. "Why CMOs Never Last." https://bit.ly/dmo-24-v

 [vi] Deloitte. "The CMO Survey." Deloitte. https://bit.ly/dmo-24-vi

Conclusion

Should You Outsource Digital Marketing or Keep it In-House?

Congratulations! You've now equipped yourself with the recipe for digital marketing success. Although we're nearing the end of our journey together, you'll soon embark upon one of your own, and I have every confidence that you're poised to do well. Before we part ways, however, I want to recap and solidify a few key takeaways from the recipe to help you put your best foot forward.

5 Questions That Will Tell You if Digital Marketing Outsourcing is Right for You

In my recipe, control of digital marketing remains in-house, at the heart of the business. Beyond that, the decision to keep individual functions or roles within the digital marketing team in-house or outsourced should be considered on their own merit. You want an expert in each area but must also balance how your team works best and budgets. These role-based decisions may be different for each organization.

This is the methodology I bring with me to each project as a business and digital marketing consultant, and it has a 100 percent success rate. You can apply this strategy by asking yourself these five questions for each role you're considering filling in-house or outsourcing.

1. Does your in-house team have the required skills and expertise?

Become familiar with the role and the necessary capabilities someone must possess to be able to perform the duties associated with it. Better yet, start by creating a list of these skills or refer to the role-based chapters in this book as you begin. If your in-house team doesn't already have the skills listed, consider how big of a challenge it would be to find someone you're certain possesses them.

For example, you may be able to gauge whether someone can write or not, but do you have the background to assess whether an SEO writer can actually create content that boosts search engine rank?

If you can't judge with accuracy, you don't have in-house talent who can already fulfill the role, or you can't easily hire someone you're sure can perform for you, it's usually better to outsource.

The only caveat here is that sometimes you need an "insider" who understands what's happening within your organization on a daily basis. So before you settle on outsourcing as your solution, consider whether you need someone with a pulse on your company and, if so, if it's possible for an outsourced provider to have one.

2. Does your in-house team have access to the right tools and the ability to use them effectively?

Secondly, create a list of tools your employee will need if you keep the role in-house or use the lists I've provided. Consider "tools" in a broad sense. An in-house writer, for example, will need a workstation and software. An in-house video production team will need that and perhaps recording equipment, props, editing software, and more.

You might be able to get a writer set up in-house, but purchasing all the tools your in-house video production team will need will become costly. If you don't have the tools and purchasing them will be cost-prohibitive, it may be better to outsource to someone who already has them.

3. Does your in-house team have the time to manage the role effectively?

The next thing to consider is how much time it takes to perform the work well. Again, identifying how much time something takes may require research. For example, you may think someone on your team can tackle your email marketing.

That person may have the skills, and you may already have tools, but remember that the "average" email campaign takes 12 hours to plan and implement. Most organizations run several per month. The time will add up, and if your internal hire doesn't have the bandwidth, they will either underperform or get burned out fast.

You'll need to hire additional staff or outsource to a third party if your in-house marketing team members don't have the capacity to do the job well.

4. Do you have KPIs and technology to measure the success of the role?

An additional consideration is how you'll measure the success of the role. For example, how will you know your marketing professional is meeting objectives? If you're drawing a blank, you should probably outsource the digital marketing role to someone who can provide you with transparency and reporting.

5. Have you run a cost analysis?

Thus far, if all things up to this point are equal, consider how much you're spending on keeping a digital marketing role in-house versus outsourcing. Oftentimes, outsourcing is more cost-effective.

For example, your in-house team might be able to use inexpensive software to make explainer videos for marketing, but if it's not really what they do, they could easily spend a full day doing something a pro might be able to complete in an hour.

Role-By-Role: Should You Outsource Digital Marketing or Keep it In-House?

Now, let's put those five questions into practice. Below, we'll revisit some of the most common digital marketing roles and you'll see how the decision is made. Using these examples, you'll be able to make informed decisions about any digital marketing role you may add in the future.

Digital Marketing Management

Digital marketing management often fails the first question on our five-point checklist because outsourced talent doesn't usually have insider knowledge. It will typically be an in-house role because of this. There are exceptions, though.

Compare how I behave as a digital marketing consultant to how most marketing agencies work, for example. I become part of the team and interact with everyone from the owners or C-suite to individual contributors. I live and breathe the brand every day. On the other hand, most outsourcing firms meet with a client a couple of times at the onset of a project. From there, they devise a strategy, tell you what they're doing, and then carry out their plan. They'll never understand a business's objectives, who its customers are, or what metrics to measure that way. They may not even know if their marketing plans are performing if they're not tuned in.

Copywriting

Copywriting is one of the few roles that can be successfully outsourced or kept in-house. I touched on the role a bit earlier. It's one that requires few tools, and the success of the role is largely based on the skill of the individual. It's possible to give an affirmative answer to all five questions in our checklist.

Do you have someone in-house who can maintain your brand voice that creates copy people read and share, and does this person have time to create a quality copy? If so, you can keep this role in-house. However, if you struggle to find someone who can meet any of these objectives, outsourcing is necessary.

Social Media Marketing

Generally speaking, social media marketing is a role you probably want to keep in-house. This is one example where the caveat outlined in the first question comes into play. Your social media person will likely not only be managing the posts but interacting with people and businesses on your behalf. They become the voice of your brand.

Moreover, there will be times when this individual must make rapid-fire decisions on how to address questions, comments, and concerns posted by your audience. To perform well, your social media marketing professional must know your brand, its voice, and what's happening with the organization on a daily basis. It's tough to find someone who can do this through outsourcing.

However, suppose you have one dedicated person working on your project who genuinely gets to know your brand and interacts with you enough to have a pulse on the business and provide the consistency your audience needs on social media. In that case, you can outsource this role too.

Search Engine Optimization (SEO)

You should probably be outsourcing SEO, as it's typically performed by several specialists. There are people who perform keyword research, analysts, strategists, on-page optimizers, off-page optimizers, and more. Hiring a full team to perform all these duties, particularly when many of the tasks don't need to be done repeatedly, would be excessive.

Moreover, people who specialize in SEO and work with it daily will do it better, more expeditiously, and cost-effectively.

Pay-Per-Click

Outsourcing PPC will usually produce better results. Suffice it to say, taking a wrong turn with your digital ads can be a costly mistake. A strong PPC professional will have many different skills, such as the ability to carry out customer and keyword research and an understanding of analytics and consumer behavior. Plus, the person should be well-versed in multiple ad platforms too.

While you may be able to hire someone to manage this all in-house, the other catch is that managing PPC for a small or mid-sized company is not generally a full-time job. It could take ten hours per week or ten hours per month. The time investment will vary based on your ad spend.

However, suppose your in-house professional is only devoting a small amount of their time to your PPC. In that case, it will be challenging for them to stay abreast of trends in PPC and keep getting you the results you deserve from your investment.

Email Marketing

Like copywriting, email marketing can go either way. The role requires all the skills associated with copywriting, plus a greater understanding of the sales process and sales optimizations, as well as an assortment of tools ranging from an email service provider to render testing software. If you have someone in-house who can do all this and has the time available to do it well, email marketing is another role you can keep in-house.

Most email service providers will also provide you with stats to measure performance too, so it's easier to tell if your team is meeting goals. However, if your internal team doesn't have the skills or time required or is not meeting objectives, you can outsource this role.

Graphic Design

Most businesses will do better outsourcing graphic design because they cannot answer the tool, time, and cost analysis questions affirmatively. Remember, the single most popular graphic design suite costs more than $7,000 per year but having this tool or something like it is required to produce professional results. Additional tools beyond this may also be required. Moreover, most businesses just getting started with digital marketing will not have enough work to keep even a part-time graphic designer busy. These things skew the cost analysis and make outsourcing a more favorable decision.

Skills may be another consideration, as you're likely to find one person creates stunning whitepapers, another makes well-crafted infographics, and another makes highly sharable social media images. When you're outsourcing, you can work with three people who shine in different ways. Although consistency between designers can become an issue, creating a style guide will help, as will shared storage of source files and finished work.

App and Website Development

Outsourcing development projects is generally best. This is one area where virtually every possible box you can check will point to outsourcing. First, the field is very specialized. It's unlikely you'll have someone on your internal marketing team with the skills necessary, and most projects require more than one type of development specialist, so you'd be hiring a team versus a single developer.

You'd also need to purchase a multitude of expensive tools, and you'd probably only use them once—during the initial build of your app or website. In other words, getting everything you need in place to carry out a single project would be overkill and not cost-effective.

Hosting

In the modern era, most small businesses don't even consider hosting their own websites. Hosting companies have done a great job of showing how easy it is to outsource the service. Even still, some businesses with a strong IT department and those already working with an IT professional may hear that it's better to keep hosting in-house.

Hosting should generally be outsourced, though. Investing in servers and infrastructure makes it cost-prohibitive to keep it in-house. You'd also have to employ a full team to have 24/7 coverage to ensure your site is always up and operable.

Video Production

For the best results, you'll want to outsource video production too. But, as I mentioned earlier, high-quality videos require a lot of expensive and specialized equipment. And while you can use inexpensive software to make catchy slideshows or explainer videos, not only will your in-house person probably do it much slower than a pro because they won't do it often, but it won't have the same professional polish.

That means you'll pay more in the long run and not get the results you otherwise would. To be fair, video production isn't usually a single person's job either. You'll need writers, videographers, animators, editors, voice actors, and more.

Creating videos in-house is a huge undertaking, and you probably won't get ROI from them that way. So if you're going to include videos in your digital marketing strategy, and you should, outsource them.

Analytics

You'll probably want to keep analytics in-house too. Although it's a highly specified role that may be challenging to fill, your data is what brings all your marketing efforts into alignment with the business goals. That naturally requires having a pulse on the organization and its daily operations as well as being tuned in and available to the team for reporting needs.

It would be remiss not to mention that the success of your digital marketing strategist, trust in the marketing team, and often marketing budget, hinge on having good data.

Selecting a Digital Marketing Agency or Partner

Chances are that you've now decided your business will be better served by outsourcing one or more marketing roles. The natural pivot for most business leaders is to select a digital marketing agency that can tie up all your loose ends for you. If this is still where your mind went, pause for a moment and think through all the different skills and resources required to successfully fulfill the role you want to outsource—the very things that led you to your decision. It's a lot to take in, right?

This is why you do not want to hire a digital marketing agency either. Remember, most agencies offer a lot of different digital marketing services, but they don't excel in any one area. As the adage goes, they're a "Jack of all trades but master of none." If you're going to outsource marketing because you can't do it all, don't give the job to someone else who can't do it all. Instead, find the right talent for each role.

Taking Your Next Steps

Digital marketing is complex and constantly evolving. The behavior of your customers will change. New technology will emerge. When you have the right people on board, they'll ensure your strategies and initiatives continue to deliver ROMI year after year. Follow the recipe you've learned here, and you'll always have the right people on board to maximize your marketing budget, deliver the returns you need, and scale your business efficiently.

About the Author

Husam Jandal is an internationally renowned business strategist and marketing consultant who helps businesses drive growth through innovative marketing and business transformation strategies.

He is a thought leader, published author, and public speaker with more than two decades of experience in the digital space (since 1999), including training Google Partners, teaching e-business at a master's level, receiving multiple Web Marketing Association Awards, and earning many rave reviews from businesses and organizations of all sizes worldwide.

Husam publishes regular insights on his website and offers complimentary consultations (time permitting) to businesses looking for rapid and sustainable growth. He also provides a free subscription to his *Digital Insights* newsletter, all of which is available through his website:

www.husamjandal.com